A BRIEF TOUR OF HIGHER CONSCIOUSNESS

A BRIEF TOUR OF HIGHER CONSCIOUSNESS

A Cosmic Book
on the Mechanics of Creation

Itzhak Bentov

Destiny Books
Rochester, Vermont

Destiny Books
One Park Street
Rochester, Vermont 05767
www.InnerTraditions.com

Destiny Books is a division of Inner Traditions International

Library of Congress Cataloging-in-Publication Data

Bentov, Itzhak.
    A brief tour of higher consciousness : a cosmic book on the
    mechanics of creation / Itzhak Bentov.— [2nd ed.].
        p.   cm.
    Rev. ed. of: A cosmic book on the mechanics of creation.
    ISBN 978-0-89281-814-3 (alk. paper)
        1. Creation—Miscellanea. 2. Consciousness—Miscellanea. I.
    Title: Cosmic book on the mechanics of creation. II. Bentov, Itzhak.
    Cosmic book on the mechanics of creation. III. Title.

    BF1999 .B3975 2000
    113—dc21
                                                    00-024448

Printed and bound by Lake Book Manufacturing

10 9 8 7 6

Acknowledgments

My sincere thanks to all the responsive and generous individuals and organizations who sent me tapes of Ben's lectures, which served as a basis for a part of this book and made it possible for me to complete it.

The comments, editing, and advice of my friends were invaluable, and I thank them sincerely.

Mirtala

Contents

Contents

* These sections have been reconstructed from Itzhak Bentov's notes and tapes and additional illustrations provided by Mirtala.

Foreword to the Second Edition
by Mirtala

When Ben began writing about his inner experiences in the 1970s, later published as *A Cosmic Book,* the general level of human consciousness caused him to disguise his material in the form of a cartoon strip: "A Co^{S}mic ^{S}trip." These drawings, which are his own, are included in this revised edition of *A Cosmic Book.*

In the 1970s, unlike today, the general public was far from being aflame with the burning need to understand such questions as: "What is happening to our planet? Are the poles about to shift? Will our sun explode? Is time an illusion in the process of dissolving?" Ben had to navigate in an atmosphere of complacent slumbering in the old paradigm of Newtonian safety.

Now, as we enter the new millennium, the consciousness of the masses is shifting and changing with lightning speed, reflecting changes in the Earth herself. This acceleration creates the inevitable need to understand ourselves and the universe from a new perspective. Therefore, it is timely to make Ben's direct experiences of higher dimensions available to the public again. As we advance by leaps and bounds into four-dimensional consciousness, there are many now who will understand and fully appreciate this material and get support for their own experiences of higher consciousness.

Ben's "cosmic journey" is an invaluable blueprint and record of changes—in the awareness and in the physical body—that occur as consciousness unfolds into its full connection with its divine origin. This record demonstrates the full potential of us, human beings, to interact with the highest levels of creation, and it brings the realization that this is where we belong. It emphasizes, again and again, that the only key to these levels is unconditional love.

Ben's drawings and the diagrams, received in his daily meditations, give a pictorial "guided tour" of the unfoldment of consciousness through interaction with energies and beings way beyond the human range. One gains the understanding and the assurance that we are an integral part of this cosmic hologram of consciousness and, in time, are destined to exist on these levels in the eternity of evolution. More than that, it demonstrates that we can be—and are—there now, as soon as the illusion of separation is dissolved.

Foreword
by Christopher Bird

After the publication of *Stalking the Wild Pendulum* in 1977, its author, Itzhak "Ben" Bentov, was asked by an interviewer why he had chosen so curious a title for his work. Replied the author: "Because everything in the universe that is visible or manifest behaves like a pendulum moving from one point of rest to another. In other words, all matter vibrates."

Bentov went on to assert that pendulums, just as they reach the culmination of their swings in one direction, and before they start back in the other, actually disappear for a minus-cularly brief period, vanishing from what passes for "reality," then reentering it.

One aim of Bentov's allusion to an evanescent quality in the pendular swing was doubtless to jolt his readers into insights beyond conventional thinking in the same way that a Zen master uses a *koan* to vault his postulants beyond the domain of "common sense" into that realm of Buddhist enlightenment known as *satori*.

It was Bentov's view that human beings themselves behave something like pendulums in that, throughout the swings of life, they build a picture of the universe on the basis of an "on-off" switching mechanism. During the "off" periods, they can expand into a region unbounded by time and space, then collapse back to continue "normal" life as if nothing extraordinary had happened. Such periods of ecstasy range from the fleeting to the more enduring.

Letters received by Bentov suggest that his readers did not find it difficult, in fact were eager, to embrace this conceit. He seemed able to affect in them a chord all too ready to resonate if plucked. The director for executive recruitment of a large international firm of certified public accountants, headquartered in New York, wrote: "Having a nonscientific but inquiring mind, your explanation of the workings of Nature gave me a better grasp of the cosmos and the relationship of human beings thereto than anything I have read to date. Thank you for opening the horizons of my mind . . . my soul . . . and please start another book."

The present short work is the evidence that Bentov heeded that injunction to produce a sequel, a task ably finished by his talented sculptress wife, Mirtala, after his untimely death.

The verb "to invent," as its Latin derivation, *invenire*, connotes, means to "come on" or, more idiomatically, to "happen on" or "come across," implying a fortuitous event or unplanned action. As a skilled plyer of the inventor's trade for much of his life, Bentov's day-to-day experience convinced him that people can visit an extracorporeal, nonmaterial province where so-called "objective" time—as measured by watches and clocks—is suspended and gives way to shorter or longer periods of "subjective" time in which one can be anywhere and do anything one wishes, limited only by creative imagination.

As far back as 1909—perhaps unknown to Bentov—the British jurist Thomas Troward, in his lectures on mental science delivered at Edinburgh University, discussed a "subjective" mind that he held to encompass all time and all space. Troward was exploring a *terra incognita* of which academic psychology is only beginning to take note. Such pioneers as Elmer and Alyce Green, of the Voluntary Controls Center at the Menninger Foundation in Topeka, Kansas, have discovered that subjects trained in meditation can attain mental states in which their brains emit waves, called *theta*, at rates between four and eight cycles per second. During this "*theta* reverie," the subjects are bombarded with hosts of vivid, often symbolic, images, occasionally so alarming as to be severely disturbing.

Bentov, it appears, came to the realization that, if the reverie were subject to willful control and focused on a specific problem, the images received would contribute to its solution. He not infrequently experienced what he termed "Ah, hah!" moments when ordinary mental processes, slipping their moorings of rationality to hoist sails into the winds of intuition, could seize prizes of pure information on the ocean of the infinite.

The act of apprehending the supersensible was, in an earlier day, attributed to *gnosis*, or intuitively revealed knowledge that, during an "age of reason," ceded its place to *scientia*, or knowledge based on sensory information and repeatable experiments. The substitution of the one for the other was complete the day Baron Verulam Viscount Saint Albans, better known as Sir Francis Bacon, announced: "Reality *only* presents itself to us when we look upon the world of the senses which *alone* provide us with realities." (Emphasis added.)

Yet, a century ago, Friedrich August Kekulé candidly confessed he had hit on the shape of the benzene ring, a discovery that laid the basis for modern organic chemistry, as a result not of painstaking work in his Ghent University laboratory but of spontaneous imagery that came to him when he was half asleep. In his report to the German Chemical Society, he urged his fellow scientists: "Gentlemen, let us learn to dream!"

A few years later, the Serbian prodigy, Nikola Tesla, whose discoveries transformed electricity from a scientific curiosity to a technological revolution, while strolling in a Budapest park was moved to declaim lines from Goethe's *Faust:*

> *The day retreats, done is the day of toil.*
> *It yonder hastes, new fields of life exploring.*
> *Ah, that a wing could lift me from the soil*
> *Upon its track to follow, follow soaring.*

The words were hardly out of his mouth when Tesla was struck by the vision of a magnetic whirlwind turning a motor. Over the next several days, he worked it up into detailed blueprints in his mind, where they remained for six years until, after his emigration to the United States, he elaborated them into the hardware that became the alternating current generator.

In our own day, a similar process of mentation was described by Arthur Young, author of *The Reflexive Universe: The Evolution of Consciousness*, and inventor of the first commercial helicopter built by Larry Bell. During a nineteen-year-long effort to crack the problem of stabilizing the rotary wing, Young came to the point where he was sure he was getting close to the solution. Why? "Because I had a *creepy feeling*," he recalls. "It was as if I were walking around a corner and expecting something to happen. Even the slightest sound made me jumpy. The first time it occurred, the air felt super-saturated. I was so sure my idea was going to work that I asked my patent attorney to witness the first flight. My model was ready to go, and almost ceremoniously I got it started. It took off and immediately turned upside down and crashed. My lawyer was so disgusted he swore he'd never come back for any more crazy demonstrations. Two or three days later the real thing came through to me. The preliminary brainwave was a false alarm. I believe it was because I was anticipating the real thing."

Dreams, visions, creepy feelings? Super-saturated air? Things being "anticipated" and finally "coming through?"

Coming through from where? Bentov's answer: from a Universal Mind containing any knowledge desired as long as the human psyche is prepared, or has prepared itself, to receive it.

As part of his own preparation, Bentov himself at first resorted to the artifice of a "wet method," meaning that he would immerse himself in a bathtub full of water as hot as he could stand, there to sit, "spaced out," often for hours at a stretch, scribbling down ideas on the leaves of a small note pad and sticking them, one by one, onto the steam-soaked tiled wall above the tub. In his relaxed "twilight zone" state, something akin to a hypnagogic dream, he was able to receive flashes of understanding that he could later synthesize into solutions to the problems preoccupying him.

Subsequently he found he could dispense with the bathtub crutch in favor of a "drier" method, that of meditation or relaxed concentration. By this means, as he put it, "I could attain remote reality by simply visualizing myself to be there, and there I was. . . ."

Among the many problems Bentov was called upon to solve for companies engaged in diverse fields of endeavor was the development of a painless hypodermic needle. Seen under magnification, the tip of a needle has four beveled edges, the configuration of which determines how effective they are in penetrating skin and flesh. Since the coring action of the needles causes the pain, Bentov, in one of his "reveries," concentrated on how Nature herself might most elegantly solve the problem. It came to him that what he should investigate was the design of the tips of the fangs of poisonous snakes, since for millennia, these reptiles seemed to have been, of all creatures, most adept at hypodermically injecting venomous fluids into their victims.

Acting on his vision, Bentov betook himself to a Florida snake ranch, where he was allowed to help himself to as many dead snakes, killed after their poison had been extracted, as he could use. After toting home a small sackful of fangs, he found, as he suspected, that Nature, way ahead of any inventor, had provided him with exactly the answer he was seeking.

In neither of his books does Bentov provide other examples of how his voyages into a continuum beyond space and time helped him in his inventor's art. Rather, they set forth a cosmology that came to him piecemeal during his practice of the "dry method" of revelation. The horizons swept in these works—which should be read in conjunction—are related to those opened by seers ranging from Jacob Boehm and Emmanuel Swedenborg at the end of the Middle Ages to Helen Blavatsky and Rudolf Steiner at the turn of the century and to the received knowledge of many other western mystics, trance mediums, and spiritually oriented visionaries before and since.

That the truths revealed are far older than their appearance in western tradition is evinced by a letter received by Bentov from a renowned authority on yoga in India, who wrote:

> What you say about the nature of the Universe is authentic . . . the "point of rest" of your "wild pendulum" is technically called "spanda" in Shaivite philosophy. It is the initial impulse, throb, *Shakti*, energy or cosmic will of the Supreme Reality. It is all-pervasive energy. What you call the "off-state" of consciousness is called *samadhi*, or the super-conscious state in the language of Yoga. It is true that instantaneous communication throughout the Universe is possible. The Ultimate Reality of Supreme Consciousness is beyond the limitations of time. Empirical time or objective time has no meaning in that state.

So categorical an affirmation, as indeed Bentov's own conclusions, will be summarily brushed aside as meaningless by materialist philosophies now rampant in the world political arena. But to those weary of the daily litany chorused in newspaper headlines, they offer new blazes on a trail into a realm beyond the mundane.

A Note on Ben
by Jean Houston, Ph.D.

In the thirteenth century, the great German mystic Meister Eckhart came to the same conclusion that Ben Bentov arrived at in the late twentieth century. He said, "The eye by which I see God is the same eye by which God sees me." Eckhart got into a lot of trouble with the Pope over that one. Bentov, however, only got us, and God, laughing in agreement. Such are the ways of progress.

In his search for the cosmic connection, Ben offers us a delightfully ingenious cosmic comedy on the nature and structure of ultimates. Here are traveler's tales such as you rarely find—metaphysical jaunts from one end of the universe to the other. He gives us back the unimaginable universe—unimagined only because the lenses of our local imagination are too limited to contain it. By opening his own lenses through intensive and consistent meditation, he entered into the field of quantum resonance wherein one can always gain access to any part of the universe.

In those unitive states of consciousness associated with mystical experience, rapture, and meditation, there is often a stilling of the mind, accompanying the regularity and slowing of brain waves into synchronized alpha and theta patterns. Sometimes the coherence of the brain's wave pattern reaches a proportion that then engages the entire brain wave pattern in resonance. This results in unbounded—and unlensed—awareness, mystical experiences, and a genre of feeling and knowing that seems to belong to a deeper order of reality.

Ben fell into the great hologram of the Way Things Work. In doing so, he discovered a perspective that is very ancient and has been known to mystics, magi, and other boundary-breaking folk for millennia. One finds an early formal description in the second-century Buddhist Avatamska Sutra:

> In the heaven of Indra there is said to be a network of pearls, so arranged that if you look at one you see all the others reflected in it, and if you move into any part of it, you set off the sound of bells that ring through every part of the network, through every part of reality.
>
> In the same way, each person, each object in the world, is not merely itself, but involves every other person and object and, in fact, on one level is every other person and object.

Similarly, the seventeenth-century philosopher Leibniz declared the universe to be made up of "monads," tiny units of mind, each of which mirrors the universe from the perspective of its particular point of view. At the same time, each component, each monad, is interrelated with every other, so that, as in Indra's net, no monad can be changed without changing every other.

In cabalistic lore, the hologram finds its occult expression in the symbol of the Aleph, the point that contains all possible points in the infinite dance of space–time.

Now if the hologrammatic-Buddhist-monadic-cabalistic-Bentovian universe is true, then you are literally ubiquitous throughout the universe and are being sent out as an interference pattern through the flow emulsion of the ether to all possible places in the matrix of space–time. Seen from this perspective, this is a universe of colossal busy-bodyness, with everybody involved with everybody else all the time. Ben never stopped laughing over that one. Seen from this perspective, too, so-called "psychic" phenomena are only byproducts of the simultaneous-everywhere-matrix. And synchronicity— those coincidental occurrences that seem to have some higher design or connectedness—would seem to derive from the purposeful, patterning, organizing nature of the Absolute.

What is more, we always have a standing invitation to join the Absolute in the co-creation of emerging evolutionary ideas and forms. That is the hot news that Ben brought back from the Center of Everywhere.

Ben was an aficionado of waves and frequencies. His own revelations were modulated through the lenses of engineering and a passion for structure. He would be the first to say that his revelations were therefore true but not accurate. He utilized the current myth of science to understand the nature of reality. His mysticism was tempered by modern metaphors. Fortunately, his own lensing was itself shattered by his outrageous sense of humor. He may have well laughed himself into Truth.

Preface

Itzhak Bentov—known simply as Ben—was an inventor, trained as a mechanical engineer. His imaginative creations covered a wide range, from paper yarn to explosives to a heart pacemaker electrode. In his last years, concentration on bio-medical engineering led him to explore the electromagnetic field around the body, which he attempted to correlate with altered states of consciousness, such as dreams or meditation. He was particularly interested in the physiological changes produced in the body by meditation. Ultimately, his practical experience as an engineer led him to develop an overview of the evolutionary pattern of humankind. He saw the human nervous system as the key to the process of evolution of consciousness, involving creative energy, or Kundalini,* which catalyzes and speeds up this process.

Ben spoke of himself as a "nuts-and-bolts man" who dealt with mechanisms and structures. The descriptive subtitles of his two books show this interest: "On the Mechanics of Consciousness"† and "On the Mechanics of Creation." This volume is a study of the nature of consciousness and its evolution in terms of expansion into ever higher levels of Creation. In

---

* A Sanskrit term for creative energy in the human body, located at the base of the spine. Its "awakening" is said to open up higher states of consciousness.

† Itzhak Bentov, *Stalking the Wild Pendulum: On the Mechanics of Consciousness* (Rochester, Vermont: Destiny Books, 1988).

meditation, Ben perceived these levels visually as ever-evolving structures, or one could say that consciousness manifested itself to him in forms that revealed its functioning on different levels. These forms were of a nature most appropriate and understandable to a man of his particular training and background.

Evolution pushes humanity toward godhood, "whether we like it or not," as Ben put it. All matter, which Ben equated with consciousness, including human beings, is on a conveyor belt moving upward, and there is no way to get off. The process of evolution of consciousness may be accelerated by meditation and other spiritual practices, but even without them, Ben would reassuringly say, "In time everybody gets there anyway."

Ben had a delightful sense of humor, which he often directed at himself: "I'm a plumber," he would reply, when asked what he did. Even when discussing lofty subjects such as the nature of reality, the cosmos, or evolution, Ben could make his audiences chuckle from beginning to end. "People take themselves too seriously," he would say, and he captured his audiences by presenting complex concepts in a simple, playful way. He radiated peace and a kind of contagious cosmic joy.

Ben liked to tell the story of how, at the age of nine, he began his search for God. Defying his Jewish background, Ben decided to test the existence of God with a ham sandwich, forbidden by his religion. Moreover, he was going to eat it on Yom Kippur, a high Jewish holiday of fasting and atonement. Eating a ham sandwich was bad enough, but on Yom Kippur, what could be more challenging to God?

In order not to endanger anybody's life (what if his deed caused the roof to collapse?), he went to the city park, sat on a bench, and bit into the sandwich. He looked up: no lightning, no brimstone. Maybe God hadn't noticed? He took another bite. Nothing. He finished his sandwich and concluded that there must be more to God than what he had been told. His lifelong search had begun.

There was nothing small about Ben. The scope of his quest was wide: Who are we? Where are we going? What is the nature and structure of reality? What is the purpose of evolution? What is consciousness? He would begin his talks by saying, "Now we will talk about all there is. From atom to cosmos. From humanhood to godhood. And that's a lot to talk about."

Jokingly, he would say, "We all are on the same bus, moving through infinity; only some have window seats, others aisle seats. I happen to have a window seat." He had a tremendous curiosity about Creation and an unusual fearlessness for exploring it. And through it all, he kept a sense of balance. In meditation, he would explore the farthest reaches of the cosmos, then return to work on a lathe or design an instrument in his lab, keeping a sound and balanced perspective on the two realities.

Ben's mind worked on two levels: As a scientist, he functioned on the objective, factual level; as a meditator, he experienced the subjective, intuitive knowledge of a mystic. The combination of these two very different, often counterpoised ways of knowing gave Ben a unique perspective on the nature of reality, and to know reality was his total commitment and message. In this way, Ben's life journey reflects the great visionaries of the past and, perhaps, anticipates the great seers of the future, combining an understanding of the material world (science) with inner, intuitive knowledge (direct cognition through higher states of consciousness).

Many people *talk* about higher states of consciousness, using inscrutable words and involved philosophical terms to explain them. Ben never used fancy words; he disliked them. He simply *lived* that higher state and felt at home in it, and whatever he said or wrote came directly from that level.

He never presumed his ideas to be any kind of final absolute teaching, and many of them he considered working models. He always emphasized, "I speak from my present level of ignorance. The more you know, the more ignorant you become, because ignorance grows exponentially—the more answers you get, the more new questions arise." Or he would say, "I'm just a tourist, snapping pictures and bringing them back to share with you." In his Introduction to *Stalking the Wild Pendulum* he wrote, "I do not claim that the information contained here is the final truth, but I hope that it will stimulate more thinking and speculation by future scientists and interested laymen."

This is the story of a soul's journey back to its true knowledge of itself, and it can only serve as an example of what is possible. Each person's experience of the path back to the source is an individual one, characterized by one's particular background.

Ben died in the DC-10 crash in Chicago in 1979, en route to a conference on the nature of consciousness. This book was in progress at that time, with parts 2, 4, and 5 almost finished, including the drawings for them. Parts 1 and 3 are a faithful reproduction of Ben's drawings and words taken from his numerous lectures, with very few additions and no interpretation given. The latter is left to the reader.

Ben was hesitant to reveal this material because of its unusual, personal nature, but finally decided that it might help some other traveler on the way. With that in mind, he began to write down his experiences.

And so he passed through our sky like a meteor, illuminating it for us in a flash and giving us a glimpse of an unusual and glorious journey.

Mirtala

Introduction

It would be good to start from the beginning, that is, with some early personal experiences. Once upon a time I was a baby. Then, after a while, I became a blacksmith. But before that, at about the age of four, I was fired from kindergarten for some alleged clandestine activities. That sealed my fate and set me on a course of random interactions with the organized educational system. But on the whole, I remained untouched by it.

From blacksmithing I went into plumbing, then became an electrician, then a foundryman, then found myself building weaponry (I had noticed that one of the periodic wars was in progress). Before I knew what was happening, I became a consulting engineer, inventing new industrial products. In industry there are lots of hard-nosed people going around with sharp-pointed pencils, figuring out costs and feasibilities, profit margins and schedules. It seems that this is what makes things go round. I was also hardnosed, used a slide rule, talked tough with facts and figures, and appeared very much like one of them. I got by on that, and they took me seriously. Then somehow, I backed into medical instrumentation and, believe it or not, started manufacturing the stuff.

Somewhere along the way I took up meditation and was drawn deeper and deeper into it. My hard nose started softening. That doesn't mean that I couldn't perform as before. I could, but there was an extra dimension added to everything I did.

Combining my background in engineering with my interest in meditation, I began to study the physiological changes induced in the human body by these heightened states of consciousness. Thus I found good use for my nuts-and-bolts background in looking at the softer end of our reality. The softer end turns out to be a lot of fun and an exciting adventure, and this is why I have decided to write about it.

This is a sequel to my previous book *Stalking the Wild Pendulum,* where I attempted to put into rational, scientific, or pseudoscientific language the subject of consciousness. Many of the concepts mentioned here are explained in that book and are not wholly reviewed here, to avoid repetition. Consciousness is too vast a subject to be squeezed into the narrow bag of science, and it became clear to me that another book needed to be written, in which the raw data or unmanicured facts relating to consciousness had to be given. So, here it is.

In *Stalking the Wild Pendulum,* I mentioned the soul in an offhand fashion, saying that it is close to something we call the psyche. But, of course, that was a serious book. In this one I'll have to stop pretending and describe things as they are.

Nowadays, in a polite society one does not talk about the soul. It's an embarrassing subject. Some poets and churchmen occasionally mention it. The man in the street, when going to church on Sunday, takes his soul out of the closet, along with the rest of his Sunday best, dusts it off, and puts on his new hat. When the services are over, back goes the soul into the closet, to accumulate another week's dust. The soul is not a practical thing; there is nothing one can do with it. It is also a rather private thing; one does not talk about it to his fellowman, because it just may turn out that the other fellow has no soul and does not know what you are talking about.

Lately the public media have invaded our privacy. Contraception is discussed in public; hemorrhoid remedies are touted over a wide electromagnetic spectrum. Why is no one promoting souls? Probably because it is difficult to make money doing it. Hence the lack of sponsors. So this book is about souls, angels, and much more.

The unfolding of consciousness is an inner, private, and intimate process, and therefore courage and a great amount of frankness will be required to reveal the process as it occurs. It is certainly much easier and safer to write a scholarly and sterile third-person scientific treatise, in which one does not get personally involved in the process. For better or worse, the plunge has to be taken.

We have to keep in mind that Creation is a big hologram. In other words, every little unit cell in the big structure, whether it is a universe, a cosmos, a super-cosmos, or a super-duper-cosmos, contains the information about the whole big structure. The smaller the unit cell, the fuzzier the information; nevertheless, it is there.

Similarly, we human beings, as part of the big structure, must contain the information about the universe in some way, just as each cell in our bodies contains the information about the whole body. This information is held and structured in our consciousness, usually in latent form. The unfolding of consciousness, that is, *spiritual evolution*, opens up this latent knowledge. Encoded in our reality, this knowledge appears at first on the threshold of consciousness as vague feelings, becoming more and more clear as spiritual evolution proceeds. Eventually, we start functioning on different levels of consciousness, or "realities," as I call them. By functioning I mean we can interact with inhabitants of other realities or systems.

Soon we find ourselves involved in a fascinating adventure, where nature unfolds the information about itself, its structure, and how it functions. Unfortunately, this process does not fit well with what science knows today. But you will find, as the book progresses, that the nature of reality is much too big a subject to be encompassed by a limited human mind and knowledge. Science deals, after all, with just a very narrow and limited aspect of human experience. The softer sciences, such as psychology and psychiatry, are scratching only the surface of the psyche. There is no comprehensive model of what we are all about, and the science of the psyche is still in its infancy. The eastern philosophies have a far broader and more inclusive model of the human being, but their language is often incomprehensible to westerners. So we won't worry about science for the time being (to say bad things about science is worse than being against motherhood) and will rely only on our own subjective experience on this trip.

At first, the material dealing with our planetary existence is experienced. It includes various beings associated with our planet. We may call them archetypes, a comfortable and reassuring word to use. Eventually, some aspects of the solar system reveal themselves, then gradually one progresses toward higher spiritual levels.

Let me point out that the emerging realities are nonphysical in nature. In *Stalking the Wild Pendulum* we talked about the nonphysical or subtle bodies as interpenetrating and extending away from the physical body. They could be described as higher harmonics of the physical body. Similarly, as consciousness unfolds, revealing *to itself* the different realities *it* contains, we find these realities also to be a hierarchy of higher harmonics of our physical reality. The lower ones resemble our own physical level, but as we rise through these levels, the experiences become more and more rarefied, resembling less and less our physical, planetary reality.

This does not mean that we can dismiss these higher realities as irrelevant to our own, only because they don't look like anything we know. These abstract realities, if we wish to call them that, contain the seed of much that eventually occurs in our reality, since events trickle down from higher to lower levels. Therefore, by dealing with those realities we can substantially influence events on our level. This is all within our capability. To put it simply, if our thought patterns are longlasting and coherent, or one-pointed, we can influence our environment. Positive thought patterns will tend to cause positive events to occur, while consistently negative ones will cause our environment to respond with negative events.

We interact with the nonmaterial realities through the higher harmonics or nonphysical components of our physical body, usually referred to as higher bodies. Let us say, for example, that we want to function in the reality just above ours. It is the emotional reality, in which we experience vivid dreams. For that purpose we would use our emotional or astral body. In order to interact with still higher realities, we would automatically pick the right vehicle or higher body. The vehicle we use always matches the reality in which we intend to function. While acting on a particular plane, the appropriate vehicle is subject to specific laws and truths of that plane.

As consciousness evolves and information starts pouring in, the information is couched in a language best understandable to the person involved. For instance, a poet will be shown the nature of Creation in poetic images, an artist in visual symbols, and a mathematician in abstract equations; a nuts-and-bolts fellow like myself will have it shown to him as *structure*. In other words, each unit cell (individual human being) in this hologram not only contains the information about Creation, but contains it in individualized, specialized form. Fortunately, since like-minded people contain it in similar forms, cross-checking of information is possible. I am lucky to have met several people whose experiences have been similar to mine, so that I have been able to compare my information with theirs. To my great surprise, our experiences agreed not only in general, but also in many unexpected details. This knowledge appears, therefore, to be consistent and *reproducible*.

You may think me very irreverent when I am discussing gods, devas, angels, and so on. The reason for this is simple. If you talk to any of these high beings and ask reverently, "Hey, mister, are you holy?" the being will look at you and say, "Why don't you go and ask my boss? He is much bigger than I; maybe he is holy. As far as I'm concerned, I just work here." Moreover, they are evolving just as we are, and they, like we, have a long way to go. I hope, then, that no one will be offended if we just talk to them in plain street language. After all, we are all part of the same hologram; all the zillions of beings are contained within our Selves, because we *are* the system. Why be sanctimonious with yourself?

With these encouraging bits of information we can now start on our cosmic journey. Please, put on your seat belts, it may be a rough ride. Preposterous as it may sound, we shall talk about nothing less than the formation and structure of our universe.

Itzhak Bentov
1978

A BRIEF TOUR OF HIGHER CONSCIOUSNESS

CO$_{\wedge}^{S}$MIC $_{\wedge}^{S}$TRIP

ADVENTURES OF A SOUL

BY:

ITZHAK BENTOV

This book was originally conceived by Ben as a comic strip about two characters going on a cosmic trip, involving Ben's own experiences. It was an attempt to talk about serious matters in a lighthearted way— certainly not a new method, whenever an author handles controversial or very personal material.

Part 1

THE FERTILE VOID

The Model of the Universe

At the end of *Stalking the Wild Pendulum,* we left the Creator of our universe hanging out there in the cold, vast void. Perhaps it would be good to begin by refreshing our memory about the Creator and His universe.*

Our universe has the shape of a torus, like an elongated hollow doughnut. In the center of it is a focal point, a consciousness, or the Creator, represented by the white and black holes back to back. The Creator is like a seed containing all the information about the universe in potential form, as the acorn contains the pattern of the oak tree.

A jet of radiation emerges from the white hole and begins to flow around the Creator, forming a skin or the surface of the torus, which is the universe. Matter is born as it issues from the white hole, at first in the form of light radiation. As it cools down, stable particles are formed—protons, neutrons, and electrons. Then helium and hydrogen gases are formed. These condense into stars with heavier elements in their core. Stars collect into clusters or galaxies, and as they die, they explode and create cosmic dust, which again condenses into new stars and planets. Everything in the entire universe, including our bodies, is made of one cosmic substance. We contain atoms from the most distant galaxies and are thus connected to the whole universe.

* See chapters 8, 9, and 10 of *Stalking the Wild Pendulum.*

13

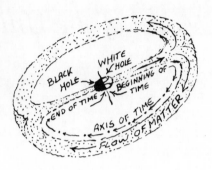

As the jet of matter continues to flow out of the white hole, it
slows down and begins to be pulled back by the gravity of the
original seed, the source in the center. The jet reverses its
direction and eventually is drawn back into the seed through
the black hole. This gravitational collapse causes matter to
become transformed into energy, as it passes from the black to
the white hole, and it reemerges from the white hole as a new
universe. It is a continuous cycle of birth and death of matter.

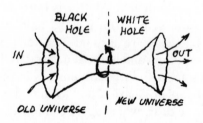

One could call it a *modest continuous bang universe*, as
compared with the Big Bang universe of a one-time explosion,
spreading evenly in all directions.

In a continuous bang universe, the white and black holes in the center of the torus are not only the points of birth and death of matter, but also the birth and death of time, for time appears where there are motion and matter. Time becomes a measure of the distance of matter from the point of its emergence from the white hole, and this distance reflects the stage of evolution of matter and its consciousness as it makes its cycle back to the source.

The universe is a hologram or interference pattern in which all parts are interconnected, containing information about each other and thus about the entire universe. As galaxies move along the surface of the torus, they radiate information waves about themselves. These waves interweave into an interference pattern and form a hologram, which fills the hollow space inside the torus, as well as extends into the surrounding void.

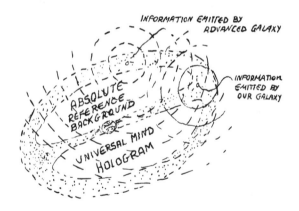

This hologram of information could be called the Universal Mind, because it contains all the information there is about the entire structure. Each individual human consciousness is part of that hologram; therefore, by projecting one's consciousness into the Universal Mind in a heightened state of awareness, one can obtain knowledge about the whole universe.

It also follows that the thoughts of all human beings are interconnected, affecting each other and in turn affecting the entire universe. Whatever one thinks or does becomes part of the universal hologram. The implications of this are obvious and far-reaching.

The Nature of the Absolute

Now let us examine the properties of the void in which the Creator and His universe are located. There are two things that can be said about the void, or the Absolute: It is *pure consciousness* and at the same time it contains all there is in *potential*, that is, nonmanifest or nontangible form. It is infinite creative energy in a potential or resting nonvibratory state. In order for matter to appear, and later for forms to appear, a vibratory motion has to be introduced into the Absolute.

Vibration means simply the movement of anything between two points of rest or two poles, as in a pendulum when it stops and reverses its direction. In other words, whatever vibrates fluctuates between its extreme poles. The movement of a pendulum can be represented by a sine wave. The crests of the waves are the points at which the pendulum stops before swinging back.

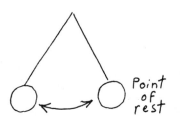

Point of rest

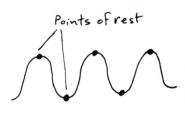

Points of rest

17

As the frequency of a wave increases, its amplitude (vertical distance between crests) becomes smaller. In other words, *the points of rest come closer together.* Imagine now a wave of such intense frequency that the points of rest come so close together they overlap, turning the sine wave into a straight line. This would represent infinite speed and total rest at the same time.

THE ABSOLUTE

In the Absolute, opposites merge and are reconciled. At infinite speed it takes no time to get anywhere; one is everywhere at once, omnipresent, in a state of total rest. The paradox is resolved.

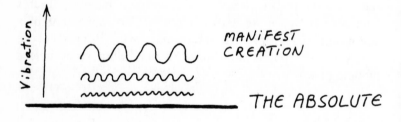

Vibration

MANIFEST CREATION

THE ABSOLUTE

Things Manifest and
Potential

To illustrate further the principle of vibration, let us imagine a soundproof room. We sit in the total silence of this room; now we take a flyswatter and start moving it through the air. As it moves, the flyswatter compresses the air ahead of it and rarefies the air behind it. This action creates two new states or a

duality in the air that has been quietly sitting there: air that is more compressed and air that is less compressed, or rarefied. The compressed and rarefied air moves away from its source, the flyswatter, in concentric waves to fill the room. As the air changes between the two states and impinges on our ears, we hear a sound. Eventually, when we stop this fascinating activity, the sound dies down. The air settles back into its previously happy, undisturbed condition, that between rarefication

and compression, and it just *is*. It reverts to a state of just
being, which is a state of unity after duality disappears.

The same happens to our void or Absolute, or pure consciousness. When it is stirred by someone or something, it
wiggles, and these wiggles spread through the void like waves
to form an electromagnetic field. When this wiggly consciousness interacts with the retina of our eye, it may appear to us as
a particle of light, or a photon. A photon is just a small piece of
this vibrating void or electromagnetic field. Now, if someone
or something insists on wiggling the void faster, then we get,
say, X rays, which are a more powerful radiation than light.
And if the void is wiggled even faster, we may get gamma rays,
which can break up into electrons and positrons, which are
particles of an atom, the basic component of matter. In other
words, this wiggly, vibrating consciousness is producing *physical matter*. It follows that the faster consciousness is vibrated,
the more matter or particles of different kinds we can get.

In short, consciousness in a vibratory state manifests itself as
our familiar matter, from which the different forms that we see
around us are made. The table, the flowers, the scent of the
flowers, and our bodies are all made of rapidly vibrating consciousness.

You may recall from your high school physics that an atom
consists of a shell of orbiting electrons with a nucleus in the
center. To get an idea of their relative sizes, visualize the
nucleus of a hydrogen atom as being about one millimeter in

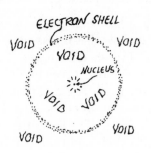

diameter, or the size of a pinhead. The size of the electron's orbit would be a circle approximately thirty feet in diameter. That is the size of a very big balloon, with the pinhead lost somewhere in its center. All the space between the nucleus and the shell is—you guessed it—void, vacuum! So, the atom is made mostly of void, which is pure consciousness, and whatever vibrates in the atom and is manifest (the electron and the nucleus) is made of vibrating void or consciousness. It is quite sobering to realize that the interstellar medium—the void between the stars and galaxies—is the same void that fills the atoms of our bodies. It is one continuous medium.

Visualize our bodies as being composed of very thin, filmy sponges. These sponges are immersed in an infinite ocean (the void), and the water is penetrating them throughout. When we, the sponges, move, the water or the void just flows through our bodies. It fills us and we are inseparable from it. This is the way things are on the microlevel, as they also are on the galactic or macrolevel. The void is everywhere, a matrix in which everything exists and which permeates everything.

Fortunately, our senses disregard all these facts and assemble lovely faces, flowers, and houses from hunks of void for us to enjoy. But we know now that our senses are deceiving us. The gruesome facts still remain. We *are* hunks of vibrating, wiggly void! Sorry about that!

The situation gets even worse if we consider the following.

As you read this book, you are thinking (we hope). Most people believe that we think with our brains. That's not quite so, but let us assume that it is. We know that our brains are made of wiggly atoms. And these wiggly atoms are made up, for the most part, of void. Right now your thinking processes are occurring on the background of the interstellar void, which is filling your brain. Consequently, your thinking consists of modifications in the vibratory processes of the void, or pure consciousness. But remember that this void is not your private void. Everybody and everything is made up of this vibrating void, whether you like it or not. Your thinking processes spread out and affect all Creation; there is no privacy, and at this point, it is too late to complain.

Now, what would happen if whoever is vibrating this consciousness ceases to do so? (Remember what happened when we stopped moving the flyswatter?) The forms that we see—and those that we are—will disappear in short order, and consciousness will come to a state of rest. It will stop fluctuating between two extremes or two poles and will revert to a happy, although monotonous, state of just *being*—pure consciousness. Everything will revert to a potential, unmanifest form. By everything we mean All-there-is, including TVs, traffic cops, rhinoceri, umbrellas, planets, washing machines, and galaxies. This is not to say those forms will stop being. They will only become potential, unmanifest cops, umbrellas, rhinoceri, and galaxies. In short, consciousness comes in two forms: vibratory and therefore manifest, or what we call matter; and nonvibratory and therefore unmanifest, but containing All-there-is in a potential state, serving as a blueprint for matter. They are two different aspects of the Absolute or pure consciousness.

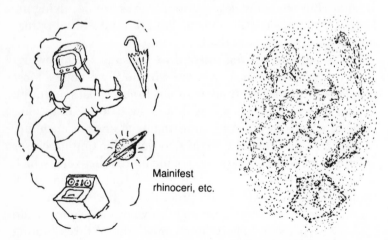

Mainifest
rhinoceri, etc.

Potential rhinoceri, etc.

Part 2

ON DEVAS, GODS, AND CREATORS

Rudimentary and Higher Consciousness

As we have seen, consciousness has two aspects, manifest and unmanifest. Let's look at our body as consciousness in manifest form and watch it in action.

Suppose you go alone at night into a bad section of town. You walk for a while; suddenly you feel a strong tap on your head. You lose consciousness. The nice fellow who tapped you on the head goes through your pockets, helping himself to your wallet, credit cards, and all the other things that are useful in this physical reality. He leaves you flat out on the sidewalk. Your breathing is slow and regular. Your heart is beating, and although your pulse is weak, it is there.

OOPS!

What has happened? *You* have lost consciousness, but your body has not. It seems to be functioning quite well and appears to have its own consciousness that directs the activity of the organs. Let us call this the *rudimentary consciousness*. It is the "wisdom of the inner parts" of the body.

Now you come to. Your consciousness, as we commonly know it, returns. The first thing you probably do is feel the lump on your head. Then you go for your wallet, but no wallet or credit cards are to be found. You start to worry and call the police.

ALTERED STATE OF
CONSCIOUSNESS

This is in great contrast to the previous situation, when your body was lying unconscious on the sidewalk. The rudimentary consciousness of the body does not seem to worry about the wallet and the credit cards. It is some other consciousness that worries about them. There appear to be two kinds of consciousness occupying our body. One is a *higher consciousness*, which is easily dislodged from our body by a relatively mild blow on the head (or by anesthesia, a less painful way of doing it). Then there is another, more rudimentary consciousness, which knows how to run a body, even when the higher consciousness is gone.

There could be, of course, a worse case. Suppose you are hit a lot harder than before. The rudimentary consciousness will do its best to keep the body going, but when it sees that the situation is beyond repair, it will also pull out and get "lost." Then you go through the process of dying, as the rudimentary consciousness extracts itself slowly from the body. Sooner or later the body becomes really dead, and both consciousnesses depart.

Let us take another example. Suppose we could project our consciousness into our kidney and strike up a conversation with a single kidney cell. We would ask the kidney cell, "Would you tell me, please, what you do here?" The kidney cell, a very simple little fellow, will probably mumble something to the effect, "Look, mister, I just work here. Why don't you ask the boss?" We go to the boss, who is the kidney itself. It is the consciousness of all the kidney cells put together. The kidney rattles off right away all the good things it is doing for the body. It tells you how it cleans the blood of harmful substances and how it regulates the components of the blood to achieve a balance among them. It is not ashamed to throw in a little bit of propaganda, just in case, saying that without the kidney we wouldn't last for very long. We are very impressed by the performance, offer our thanks for the explanation, and turn to the liver. The same thing happens: The single cell turns out to be relatively ignorant, while the composite consciousness of all the cells of the liver is an intelligent being and an expert in its field. And it had well better be. Our bodies could not function if our organs were incompetent and did not know what they were doing.

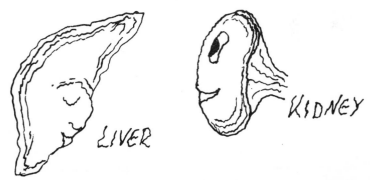

LIVER
KIDNEY

Now, if we put together the consciousness of all the organs in our body, including consciousness of the bones, skin, blood, et cetera, we end up with a very intelligent being who is the total consciousness of all the living cells in our body. This is the rudimentary consciousness, which runs the body when we are out—that is, lose consciousness—or are asleep or, for that matter, awake.

But then, what about the higher consciousness that worries about the lost wallet, telephone bills, and income tax? This is a being superimposed on the body and using it as a vehicle to experience this physical reality. It is using this body of ours to carry around our sensory mechanisms.

Our senses, as we know, give us the impressions that inform us about our environment. They use a Morse code of clicks and silences that they send to our brain-mind to describe our physical reality. The activity of a nerve cell can be represented by a series of spikes arising from a horizontal line, which represents the rest state of the nerve cell. When the nerve cell is stimulated, it produces an electric pulse or spike, the number and closeness of spikes reflecting the intensity of the stimulus. This action-and-rest activity of the nerve cell expresses the vibratory nature of reality.

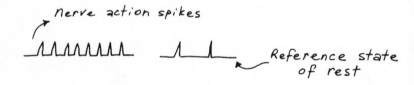

Having received these signals, the brain-mind goes about interpreting them into a picture of reality, which includes the wallet and the telephone bills. And also, of course, lovely faces, flowers, landscapes, and all else—our total environment.*

* See chapter 3 of *Stalking the Wild Pendulum*.

To sum up, we can say that we are made of two beings. One is the rudimentary consciousness of the body, which *is* the body and knows all about it. The other is the higher consciousness, which inhabits this body and exploits it for its own use. The latter is a more intelligent consciousness; it acts as an "observer," includes our mind, interprets our sensory experiences, and gives us our *self-awareness* as individuals. Let us temporarily call it the *soul*.

The soul, like everything else, keeps evolving. It may sound strange that an abstract concept, such as a soul, evolves, but on its level the soul is not an abstract concept at all. In its own reality, the soul is quite tangible. As far as we are concerned, the soul, which contains all our emotional, mental, and intuitive equipment, is the *experiencer*.* It experiences through the physical body, which is its tool for interaction on the physical level in order to learn. This does not mean that the soul cannot function without a physical body. It can and does very well. It's a being in its own right.

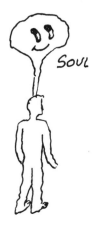

* See chapter 6 of *Stalking the Wild Pendulum*.

The information obtained from the learning process is temporarily deposited within the soul. Eventually, after being properly processed and reduced to essentials, some of it is sent off to the "boss" or the higher aspect of the soul, which we may call the Higher Self. This is an even more abstract entity, but if one interacts with it on its own level, it ceases to be abstract and becomes quite tangible. Above the Higher Self is another aspect of the soul, the Supreme Self, which is also interested in the information coming from the physical body. However, to talk about it at this point would be like telling the punch line before the joke.

The Devas

We can apply the principle of two types of consciousness to other systems. For example, think of our planet as a big body, consisting of a mass of minerals, organic matter, water, and so on. The total consciousness of its atoms constitutes the rudimentary consciousness of this body—the being that *is* the physical planet. Then we can also say that there must be

someone occupying this big body, just as the soul occupies our physical body. There is a consciousness, to be sure a very big one, that is the higher consciousness, the observer or soul of this planet. This big being (it must be big, otherwise it would not need a body the size of a planet) can be called for all intents and purposes the soul or the God of our planet. We, human beings, are part of this large being. We are contained within its consciousness, as are all the animal species and the beings that have no physical bodies.

Now consider our solar system. The sun is a very big mass of hot gas. It is several hundred times the mass of all the planets put together. So naturally it is a big body of consciousness.

Its rudimentary consciousness contains the rudimentary consciousnesses of all the planets, just as our bodies contain the rudimentary consciousness of all our organs. This large body is also occupied by a higher consciousness, which uses it as a temporary focus or garage. This higher consciousness contains within it all the planetary gods and is in charge of them and of the whole solar system.

The name given to a being that is the rudimentary consciousness of any structure is *deva*. This is a good short word that means *god* of a form. For instance, there is a deva of a tree, a mountain, or a bottle of ginger ale. Sometimes these beings are visible to persons with developed sight.

DEVA OF GINGER ALE

DEVA OF A MOUNTAIN

A mass of air or water contains so many molecules. The sum of these molecules is a deva, a being. So, we have a deva of the wind, or of the sea. Just like the deva of a mountain, they are the consciousness of the matter composing them. The fun is that you can talk to devas. You address them as "Miss So-and-So," because all the devas of Creation are female. You say, "Miss Air-Deva, can you do me a favor and pull out to sea?" You can make a deal and prevent a snowstorm in your area.

Or take ants. They are such an intelligent, organized community, but if you examine the nervous system of an ant, it's very simple—there may be six nerve ganglia or so in all. How can they behave so intelligently? It turns out that a single ant is not very smart at all, but the great intelligence of the ant colony is the deva, the total consciousness of millions of ants, the god who is a big six-foot-tall ant, and you can ask her to remove her body (the little ants) from your favorite chocolate cookie jar. To negotiate with her, the currency of exchange is love. Just send the ant deva a lot of love, which will stimulate her evolution. Even ant devas need love, in order eventually to know their Creator.

Our physical bodies are also represented by a deva, sometimes called the *lower self,* which is the rudimentary consciousness we have been discussing. Occasionally, there is a conflict between the lower self and the higher self, as in the case of suicide. The emotional and possibly the rational parts of the higher self say, "Enough. I want to die." (This is said in the mistaken belief that "all will be over," which is not the case. Consciousness goes on even without the physical body. In fact, the same emotional problems become even stronger.) The person whose higher self has decided to end it all marches off to a nearby bridge and jumps into the water. But now the lower self or the deva of the body steps in. The body will struggle for air, try to swim and get out of the water, while the emotional and the rational selves will try to sink it. The person either drowns or comes out of the experience if not wiser, then at least soaking wet.

Let us return to the larger picture. We have the deva of the sun, or the consciousness of its form, and the god, the observer or higher consciousness of the sun, who runs the solar system. A conglomeration of stars (suns), called a galaxy, contains about 100 billion stars, give or take a few billion. That is a very large being indeed, and sure enough, there are a deva and an observer who run the galaxy, which, we must admit, is a truly big job.

Devas are territorial creatures, bounded more or less by the size of the form or territory they occupy. This is not unlike animals who do their thing on bushes and posts to proclaim ownership of their territory, which is somewhat an extension of their bodies, and they protect their property jealously. So do the devas. The moment you approach their domain, they appear and question your intentions, sometimes in a manner not altogether friendly. Let us see what an encounter with the deva of a galaxy would be like.

Suppose you can expand your consciousness to encompass our sun. Once this is accomplished, keep inflating yourself until you contain many stars. Keep inflating yourself until you are encompassing our entire galaxy, a disklike collection of stars, a structure (being) with a blob of stars in its center. To do this properly, you have to feel your body as the void, and the stars as pinpoints on your body. You can zero in on any star in your body and feel it, observe it, and love it. (That is a lot of stars to love.)

Now you have expanded your consciousness to the size of a galaxy; in effect, you *are* the galaxy. Wiggle your body. This causes a disturbance, a vibration, to spread through the galaxy. (This is similar to a fly falling into a spider web. The vibration of the web signals the spider and it shows up to investigate its dinner.) The deva of the galaxy appears immediately, looking worried and saying something like "What do you want?" or "Who are you?"

You apologize for causing the disturbance and explain that you are just a tourist passing by, meaning no harm.

"Well, okay," says the deva. "So, what's new on your measly little planet?"

"I guess," you say, "the weather has been rough lately." (One can never go wrong talking about the weather.)

Sure enough, the deva relaxes and becomes more friendly. She performs a little welcoming ceremony (a *puja*, they call it) by lighting a fire and mumbling something.

DEVA OF THE
GALAXY

"How about working for me?" she says.

"No, thank you," you answer politely, "I'm on vacation and would like to do some more sightseeing."

"Well," she says, "if you ever need a job, just call. I have a job opening for you."

You thank the deva profusely, bow deeply and try to memorize her phone number and location, and then take off into the void.

Mr. and Mrs. Creator
and the
Making of a Universe

Continuing through all the innumerable galaxies making up our universe, you finally arrive at a being who *is* the universe. He contains All-there-is in our system and therefore deserves serious attention.

The boss of the universe, the Creator, is in the business of making universes; it's His profession. We will try to describe how He creates a universe, although this sounds rather preposterous. How can anyone describe anything that happened before he (we) was created? But remember that whatever happens anywhere, anytime, is embedded in the hologram, the Universal Mind. Each of us is a part, admittedly a small one, of that hologram and contains all the information about the total structure, including the information about its origin. It is just a matter of unfolding this knowledge, which is structured in our consciousness.

Now let us try to describe the process of the creation of our universe. It starts as one part of the infinite expanse of the dark void begins to stir and becomes individualized: Our Creator, having sat in the void in unmanifest form for a long time, contemplating, has finally decided to move and become manifest, in order to evolve.

After He has gone through the red tape and hassles involved in obtaining a building permit and has picked a volume of void

from the powers that be as a suitable place to build His universe, the Creator outlines a part of the void by enveloping it in an ovoid (egg shape) of golden light. He settles down to think things over and design His universe, or what is to be His manifest body. He is designing the evolution of His new body and is picking the laws of nature that are best suited to His development.

Creators are great beings, they are large consciousnesses, and they appear in three forms: (1) unmanifest form, appearing only as a powerful source of light; (2) manifest, unfurled form, that is, in the form of an active physical universe; and (3) occasionally approximating the human form. They take the latter shape simply for the sake of convenience, to communicate with human beings. A Creator may also manifest Himself simultaneously in all three forms.

Some of you may be irritated by our calling the Creator "He." The Creator is really neither "He" nor "She," but rather a He/She, male and female being, containing two polarities. It is only in lower states of consciousness that male and female are separate beings. We called the Creator "He" because we couldn't bring ourselves to call Him "It," nor could we call Him "Chairperson of the Universe."

Mr. and Mrs. Creator are two aspects of one Creator. To activate the process of evolution, they have to separate and move into opposite ends of the cosmic egg. The dynamics of Creation is based on the interaction of the negative and positive polarities. Once separated, they want to come together again, because opposite polarities attract each other. The whole cosmic egg is shaking with tension from this separation. Then the positive end extends; with a thunderous sound, the first sound of Creation, it reaches the negative end, whose protospace then begins to flow along the sides of the ovoid, like a wave, outlining the area where space-time and matter will eventually be. The Creator moves into the center of the egg, matter fills the matrix or pattern established by protospace, and action—evolution—begins.*

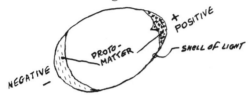

THE EVOLUTION OF THE UNIVERSAL EGG

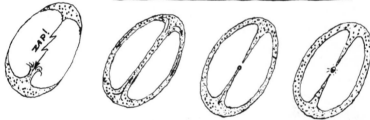

As always, there are analogies between the macro- and the microlevels. If we take a chicken egg and attach electrodes to the two ends, we discover that it reflects the structure of the universe. The two electrodes register a voltage of 2.4 millivolts, indicating an electric current running between the two ends of the egg. The chicken embryo's spine develops along the line of this current. Every seed in nature, whether plant or animal, has a similar current running along its axis, creating an electromagnetic field around the seed.

* For a detailed description see chapter 10 of *Stalking the Wild Pendulum.*

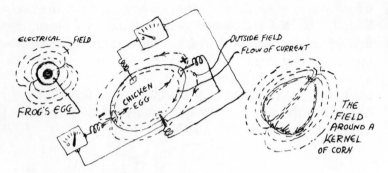

Biologists have called this current the *organizing field* of life, which guides atoms and molecules of a growing organism into their proper positions. In other words, an electromagnetic hologram or an energy pattern preexists and determines the material form, which eventually fills this pattern.

To continue our story of Creation, let us see what happens after the positive and negative polarities reunite. They continue to perform separate functions: Mr. Creator is the male, active principle, involved in the evolution of consciousness; while Mrs. Creator is the feminine principle, the Mother-Nature, the deva of all forms. All the nature devas—of galaxies, solar systems, and planets—come from Her body. She projects everything that exists, visible and invisible, into being. She is the earth, the form of the planet. She projects continents, islands, mountains, trees, and ever smaller and smaller devas of flowers and cells, down to the atom. This is how forms arise—Mother-Nature projects all forms in a hierarchy of sizes. Every atom, the whole Creation, is the body of Mother-Nature.

Part 3

BEYOND THE UNIVERSE

The Cosmos

Having seen the structure of the universe and understood its functioning, you ask, "And what's beyond this?" Immediately, you have a sensation—your consciousness, that is—of moving like a dot through the void at infinite speed without interference or impediment. Actually, you are not moving; you are filling the void with your consciousness and your senses. There is no limit to the extent of human consciousness. It can expand to fill the universe, and then you can talk to the Creator. You can talk to all the beings, who are gods; you have a diplomatic visa to infinity.

The more you expand your consciousness, the faster your sense of motion. You can expand at an infinite speed in all directions, or you can expand in only one direction. At infinite speeds, distances make no difference: You can be everywhere in no time; you are in all places at once. Our perception of time changes in altered states of consciousness, and our so-called subjective time becomes longer and reaches infinity as consciousness expands. Let us look at this principle more closely. *

There appear to be two kinds of time: *objective time*, the usual clock-time, conveniently divided into even units, and *subjective time*, a more flexible time, that can stretch and compress according to our state of consciousness. We know that in an altered state of consciousness, such as a dream, we can experience an enormous amount of events in only a few minutes. Time seems to expand, and for every objective second, one has hundreds of subjective seconds.

* See chapter 4 in *Stalking the Wild Pendulum*.

43

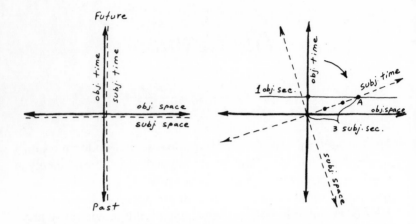

Let us draw two lines intersecting at right angles, the vertical line representing objective time, and the horizontal, objective space. Superimposed on them are two dotted lines representing subjective space-time (*left*, in figure). Under normal conditions, these two sets of lines overlap. However, in altered states of consciousness, the subjective space-time deviates from the objective space-time.

Let us mark off one second on the objective time axis and through this point draw a line parallel to the space axis. Now let us rotate the subjective time axis until it intersects with this line at point A (*right*, in figure). The point of intersection will indicate the subjective time equivalent to one objective second. We can readily see that subjective time appears to grow longer as the deviation increases. In this case, we get three subjective seconds for one objective second.

Imagine now a situation in which the subjective time axis deviates so far that it becomes parallel to and overlaps objective space. This would imply that our subjective time fills all objective space—it takes no time to go anywhere. This is what happens in expansion of consciousness: We can fill the entire universe with our consciousness at infinite speed and be everywhere at once—in other words, become *omnipresent*.

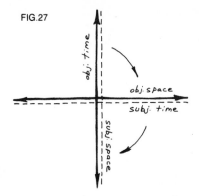

FIG.27

So here you are, seemingly moving at infinite speed in the dark void. You are leaving this universe of ours, which now looks like a luminous watermelon in the distance. You look up. In disbelief, you begin to see . . . more universes! They appear arranged in a rising spiral (helix), and you discern seven rings, each containing seven universes, or forty-nine in all. Each universe is the body of a Creator.

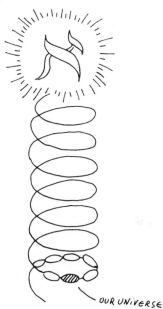

OUR UNIVERSE

God is too complex a being for us to understand, so, for our benefit, He projects Himself into three aspects, making a tetrahedron of Himself. (The tetrahedron, a pyramid with four triangular sides, is the most basic, economical, stable three-dimensional structure in the universe.) This is why most religions have trinities—the Father, the Son, and the Holy Spirit of Christianity, or Brahma, Vishnu, and Shiva of Hinduism. It's easier for us to deal with one aspect of Him at a time. Each part of such a trinity functions independently, in its own characteristic way, when it communicates with smaller consciousnesses, such as ours.

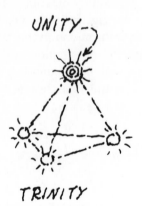

You are, then, looking at a coil of forty-nine universes. You must forget sizes and switch your scale. Imagine that you go to a gas station and inflate yourself with the air pump to the size of the gas station, then a continent, then a planet. Finally, your body is the size of the universe on this spiral, a tiny speck in the void. You must measure things in terms of universes, otherwise you would become disoriented and lose your perspective.

Above the coil of forty-nine universes you see a luminous three-dimensional form that seems made of bluish neon tubes.

Tremendous energies are flowing out of it. You are puzzled, because you recognize this as the Aleph, the first letter of the Hebrew alphabet, and you ask what it means. The explanation comes immediately, as if from someone guiding you on this tour: The shape of the Aleph has nothing to do with Jews or the Hebrew alphabet. It is an abstract three-dimensional shape formed by four creative energies that are active on this level. As the four energies of different frequencies interact, they create a rectangular interference pattern, which was directly cognized by ancient Hebrew seers and incorporated into their alphabet. The rectangular shape of other Hebrew letters also reflects this interference pattern. As we shall see later, there are other letters and symbols in space. They are part of human consciousness and therefore became the archetypal symbols of mankind.

At this level you understand the meaning and power of sounds, and how they affect the space around them. Letters, numbers, and sounds are equivalent. They all have certain effects on Creation, and you can create with any of them.

The Aleph (pronounced *Ah*) is the basic sound in the universe. It comes from lungs unobstructed. There is no other sound produced this way. The Aleph represents this whole structure, and therefore it is The All. Expressed in their corresponding numbers, the letters of The All total 50. In other words, the Aleph contains all 49 Creators or is the sum total consciousness of the Creators, since consciousness is cumulative. (49 plus the Aleph itself equals 50.)

The front side of the Aleph is luminous and the back side is dark. This expresses two polarities. From the luminous side

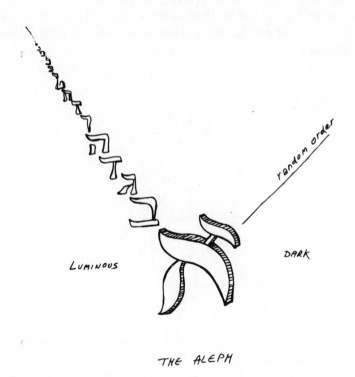

THE ALEPH

emerges a stream of twenty-two interference patterns of Hebrew letters, in the correct order of the alphabet, hovering in space; on the black side, the twenty-two letters are in a jumbled sequence. You are puzzled and wonder what this means. The explanation comes:

The interference patterns, or letters, are the transducers of the energy emanating from the Aleph, stepping it down to the physical level. On this level, good and evil exist in terms of knowledge of the law (expressed by the correct sequence of patterns) and ignorance of the law, or chaos (expressed by the jumbled order of patterns). And what *is* the law? The answer comes after seeing the entire structure.

The Aleph is broken down into three aspects or focal points, forming a trinity. They appear as groups of Hebrew letters יה, בכ, and יחב. The יה center stands for Love; בכ stands for Will, and יחב for Creation. These are the three chakras or energy centers of the Aleph, which itself stands for Wisdom.

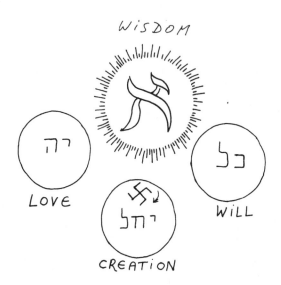

Each center radiates light of a different color, expressing the quality of energy of each particular center: gold for Love, blue for Will, and red for Creation. The Aleph radiates a brilliant white light, which is a combination of these three colors. Together, these four colors or frequencies represent the four energies that create the interference patterns of Hebrew letters.

The three centers of the Aleph can be expressed in numbers, corresponding to the letters of the centers, because in the Hebrew alphabet each letter has a numerical value. In other words, this structure is modular, built up of cycles, each represented by a unit, a number. The combinations of these units or letters express the laws of this level of Creation in an ingenious way.

The roots of many Hebrew words can be read in two directions, from right to left and from left to right, producing opposite meanings. This appears to be the case here. If the letters בל , representing the Will center, are read from right to left, toward the Love center ר ה , together they become בלידה, meaning *extinction, destruction*. If read the other way, from the Love to the Will center, they become ה ילד , which literally means "he kept walking." In other words, the general meaning is *to go, keep walking*. The cosmic law conveyed this way is that to go from love to will is all right and safe. However, if you go from will to love, you are destroying, because you must know love first. The whole system runs on love. *Love is the cosmic law.*

The letters of the creative center ריחל mean *to hope intensely, to desire*. They also mean *will begin*. Read backwards, they become בל מ ר , meaning, in essence, *for life*. Read in both directions they combine into the meaning *desire for life to begin*. This desire resulted in the process of creation, symbolized by the swastika* within the creative center, repre-

---

* The swastika is an archetypal symbol used universally by mankind since antiquity to express cosmic energy.

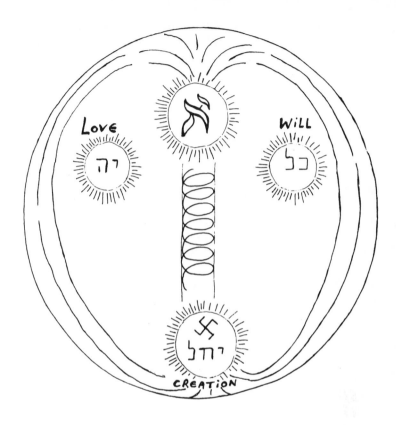

senting a four-dimensional rotating universe. It is interesting to note that if you merge your consciousness with that of the Creator, you discover within Him a rotating swastika. In other words, swastika stands for both the Creator and the Creation—they are inseparable.

Having examined and understood the details of this structure, you want to see where it ends, and going away from it, you suddenly come to a wall, which appears to have alternating flat and curved parts. You wonder why, and as you move along this wall, you realize that you are trapped within an enormous sphere. Let us call it a cosmos. You keep moving inside the cosmos, until finally you break through its luminous golden skin. To your amazement, you discover that it is surrounded by more cosmoses, each with an Aleph and a coil of forty-nine universes within, pressing against other innumerable cosmoses, like frogs' eggs.

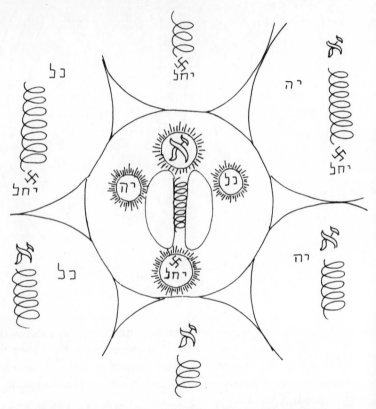

In biology there is a close-packed structure found in living cells, where only six cells can fit around a central cell, creating a tight structure of seven cells in one plane. As the cells press against each other their sides flatten in the areas of contact. This explains, by analogy, the alternating flat and curved areas in the wall of the cosmos.

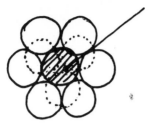

TOP VIEW

How many spheres of the same size can one put on top of these seven spheres so that they are stably located? There is space for three. On top of the three spheres, one can put only one sphere. This creates a three-dimensional module based on the tetrahedron, reflecting the numbers of spheres in each layer: 1–3–7. Two such modules joined together produce a unit cell, like a crystal.

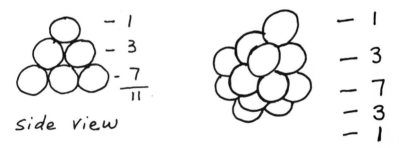

In physics, 1/137 is known as the fine structure constant, which determines the size of atoms, crystals, mountains, or whatever is structural. In relation to the cosmic module it represents one fraction of the universe. (To be more specific, the fine structure constant is a measure of the strength of the electromagnetic force that acts between the electron and the atomic nucleus and thus determines the magnitude of the electron orbit, which in turn defines the size of the atom. The structure of a material is determined by the size of its atoms.)

The whole system is built on modular forms, the tetrahedron being the basic structure of the universe. The diamond, whose structure is based on the tetrahedron, is the strongest material known, since it reflects the basic structure projected from the closely packed forms of the cosmos. This is also why, when yogis put themselves into a lotus posture creating a tetrahedron, they become the best antennae to resonate with the cosmic input of information and energy.

On levels beyond the universe, human bodies no longer appear. A consciousness that wants to project information to you will assume human features—eyes or a face—to show that it is a consciousness, something that can interact with you. For example, when you leave our universe, a consciousness shows up immediately that looks like a triangle surrounded by

AGNI

flames. Then a face appears within the triangle. The flames around it represent the four fires or energies projected by the Aleph within the cosmos. You are told that this figure is named Agni, and he appears to be the guardian of the space within the cosmos. As we shall see later, the hierarchy of consciousnesses is represented by a variety of abstract archetypal symbols.

The Super-Cosmos

What is beyond the cosmos? We human beings always want to
see the edges or the end of things. It is difficult for us to deal
with infinity.

Your body, now the size of a cosmos, continues to expand,
and all you see are closely packed structures containing Alephs
and all the rest—hundreds of thousands of them, everywhere!

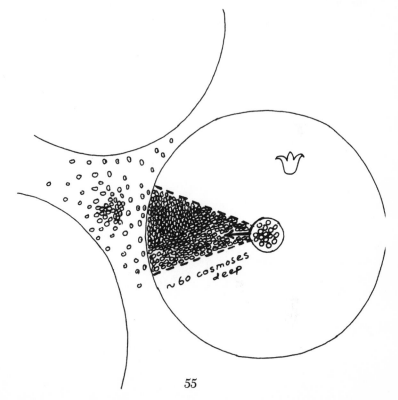

~60 cosmoses deep

Finally, you pop up on the surface. The horizon is curved, indicating that it's a sphere. You have emerged on the next level of Creation and are looking at a being—a sphere—that contains all the innumerable cosmoses. Let us call it a super-cosmos. You ask for the consciousness that runs this structure. It immediately appears and looks like a lily flower. Its consciousness contains the consciousnesses of all the Alephs, which are within it. You can talk to it. You ask the super-cosmos how it functions, and it says, "Just watch me."

Then you notice in the middle of this sphere a hollow space, five to six cosmoses in diameter, where tremendous angel beings are building shells of cosmoses. It's a factory, like those in Detroit producing cars, which will later need drivers. Just as a biological cell has its DNA manufactured and assembled by the messenger RNA, which scavenges around, picking up pieces of material for the DNA, similarly, inside the super-cosmos, golden cosmic shells are assembled. They contain no consciousness and will require a crew of Creators to run them. When a shell is ready, it is pushed out into the interior of the super-cosmos to make its way up toward the surface.

Why Evolution?

So here you are, inside the super-cosmos filled with cosmoses, about half a million of them, and you wonder what it's all about.

Suddenly you see a messenger going through all the cosmoses. As he comes to each Aleph, he says, "You have been sitting here for eons, occupying space. Have you paid your rent? We need Creators for universes in new cosmoses." The Aleph then turns to His Creators, who are working hard on their evolution, each projecting His body and climbing up the spiral.

This brings us to the crux of the question about evolution: *Why?* What's wrong with going backward, or just sitting there? The answer is that evolution is needed by the Aleph, because evolved consciousnesses are a kind of cosmic currency with which He can pay His rent. The Aleph pushes evolution and in turn, each Creator is pushing it to produce at least one consciousness good enough to run a universe, a being as good as the Creator Himself. He is making Himself in His image. Of course, evolution does not end with the cosmos. It continues into ever higher levels as consciousness unfolds to know itself. On the level of the cosmos, however, it is the Aleph that is responsible for evolution.

The universe is a machine for the distillation of consciousness. When a Creator runs His universe, it could be described as distilling a column of consciousness to raise it to a level equal to His own. Consciousness evolves; it leaves the primordial soup and gradually develops, and every now and then there is one individualized consciousness that is much better than the others. At some point it begins to reflect, "Maybe I belong to a larger structure and can figure out how this whole thing works." Then it realizes: "I reflect the Creator." At that point the Creator says, "Come here, I have chores for you to do." The whole system is designed so that the more a consciousness learns, the more responsibility it gets, and the more troubles go with it, because it has more to control.

The coil of universes in a cosmos is a coil of information, because Creators generate a lot of information as they evolve and learn. We can think of the coil as the DNA spiral of a cosmos. Those knowledgeable in electronics can also see it as an inductivecapacitive and resistive circuit, which may be used to communicate with other cosmoses, just as the DNA communicates with other cells. When the DNA of a cell replicates itself, it splits in half. The coil of the cosmos also splits in half. Each Creator pays His real estate tax by creating His double. These doubles, in turn, are used by the Aleph to pay His rent by providing crews for new cosmoses, as He delivers the new forty-nine Creators to the messenger.

The evolution of Alephs starts at the center of the super-cosmos. As their level of consciousness rises, they move up toward the surface. Our universe is located in a cosmos two-thirds of the way up in a super-cosmos. (That position should make us feel better about being in a universe at the bottom of the spiral of our cosmos.) When a super-cosmos reaches a critical dimension, it stops growing. For each new cosmos coming out of the factory in the center, one cosmos pops off the surface into the void. Around mature super-cosmoses, you can see many clouds of little cosmoses, like a mist. They collect into islands and elbow away the big super-cosmoses, forming new super-cosmoses. There is no end to it! The whole structure is a growing, living being. You realize that you are in the middle of an organism and you want to get out, to see the end.

The Manifest Creation or All-There-Is

As you move out of the super-cosmoses, you discover that there are spheres within spheres within spheres: seven levels in all. Each level is represented by a consciousness appearing as an abstract form, and these forms have become the archetypal symbols of mankind: a lily flower for a super-cosmos, an ankh for a super-duper-cosmos, next a cross, then a triangle, followed by an inverted triangle. Then the two triangles are superimposed, forming a star, and finally, on the seventh level, a human form appears, the first to represent a cosmic hierarchy. It looks exactly like an Egyptian pharaoh: a rigid figure of golden color, seated on a straight-backed chair, his hands resting on his knees.

The Egyptians must have reached this level of consciousness and borrowed this image, in the hope—not without reason—that through a sympathetic resonance with the spiritual hierarchy, they would derive power from their pharaoh, who would act as an antenna for spiritual energies.

In order to experience reality on that level, you ask the

consciousness that looks like the pharaoh, "May I go into your body and look out through your eyes?" You get permission and discover that inside he is white and black—polarities again! All you can see through his eyes are more pharaohs. He communicates with his own level, which, regrettably, you cannot understand.

The seven levels of spheres within spheres represent the seven cosmic hierarchies. The consciousnesses expressing each level are modular; that is, each contains all the consciousnesses below it.

A super-cosmos contains about half a million cosmoses. The next level, the super-duper-cosmos, contains fewer super-cosmoses, the next level still fewer, and so on. There are fewer and fewer spheres on each level, but they increase in size as you progress. You now see more in scale but less in detail. Things get simpler and simpler; information becomes condensed into symbolic forms. On earth, we use language that takes a long time to get ideas across. On a higher level, a symbol such as a tetrahedron is thrown at you and right away you know and understand all that it would take hours to explain. Our human nervous system can encompass all this and beyond.

As you go through bigger and bigger structures, you finally come to the real end—a tremendous, luminous bluish sphere, containing All-there-is, shimmering in the dark void. This is the *Manifest Creation*. All forms, physical and nonphysical, are contained within it. All that was ever created is here—all the millions and billions of Creators and universes, cosmoses and super-cosmoses, with all the beings human and nonhuman. It floats in the void, and there is absolutely nothing you can do with it. You can't tax it; you can't make money on it. It just sits there.

The Manifest Creation is made up of anything and everything that vibrates. Beyond it is the void, the Absolute, or pure consciousness, which is nonvibratory, containing everything in

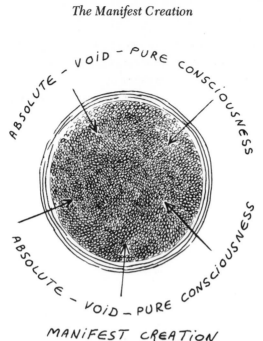

ABSOLUTE - VOID - PURE CONSCIOUSNESS

ABSOLUTE - VOID - PURE CONSCIOUSNESS

MANIFEST CREATION

its potential state. As soon as the Absolute vibrates, it manifests as Creation. Basically, they are one and the same.

Within the sphere of Manifest Creation, communication is instantaneous. Whatever you do is known immediately throughout the whole Creation, because it is such a tight structure, a hologram, with all parts interrelated. This is the basis for the law of karma or the principle that to every action there is a corresponding reaction. The whole Manifest Creation is affected by and reacts to our thoughts and actions.

The Manifest Creation is constantly growing and expanding. It is a living organism, whose every atom is filled and permeated by the void or pure consciousness. As you approach it more closely, you see that its surface is covered by what appear to be rotating disks. Then you discover that these forms resemble Sanskrit letters, with straight lines on top and wiggly lines underneath. There are three layers of those fifty-two rotating

forms or letters covering the surface. As the straight top lines
rotate, they look like rotating disks. Like the Hebrew letters,
these cosmic shapes were seen by man in an expanded state
of consciousness and incorporated into the Sanskrit alphabet.
The fourth, outermost layer is made up of forms that represent
the OM.

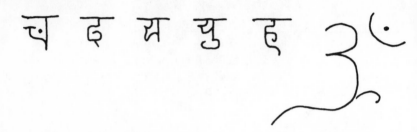

What is the meaning of these rotating forms? You are given
to understand that as the sphere expands, its surface extends
further and further into the void, which flows through the four
layers of letters. Their function is to modulate the void, like a
flute, to make it vibratory, to produce the first sound of Creation. This is the first word, and its first letter is OM. As pure
consciousness flows through the three layers of Sanskrit letters
or modulators (gunas),* they impart certain tendencies to
consciousness, making it vibratory. As the different vibrations
interact, they create an interference pattern, a hologram of
sounds, filling the whole Manifest Creation with infinite varia-
tions and reverberations of the original sound.

At the surface boundary line, the first basic structures found
in nature are produced, the primordial archetypal forms, created by the interaction of the creative word with itself. Just
below the letters, Creation is very plastic and can be manipu-

---

* According to Hindu teachings, gunas are the three tendencies in Creation—*sattwa, tamas,* and *raja*—producing the effects of expansion, con-
traction, and energy (or activity, inertia, and balance), respectively.

lated. The so-called supernatural powers of the yogis come from the siddhi level, which is located here. If you can raise your level of consciousness to this level and put in a desire, it will be manifested somewhere inside the Manifest Creation. Infinite energy comes in at this level, and you can manifest it into anything you want. This is what Jesus did when he manifested fishes and bread.

As the Manifest Creation grows, owing to new cosmoses being produced, more and more complex forms are created as the combinations and permutations of sound frequencies increase. At first it is sound; then it becomes light, then form.

Having seen all this, you are again faced with the question: Where do you go from here? And what other surprises are there in store for you?

Part 4

A GUIDED TOUR OF NIRVANA

Encounter With Naga

You are now floating in the dark void. Below is Manifest Creation, a translucent, shimmering sphere containing All-there-is and appearing like a small lost balloon in the vastness of the infinite void.

Suddenly you notice a dot of light in the darkness and you move quickly to investigate. It looks like a barred window, with light coming through it. You move in closer. A beautiful, warm light and vibrations of love are pouring out through the window. Naturally, you want to go in, but, unfortunately, the head of an enormous snake shows up in the window. He hisses and says in snake language, "What do you want?"

"Well," you say, "I'm just a tourist, interested in finding out what this is all about."

"Well," says the snake, "this is Nirvana, and once you get in, you can't get out. So, do you really want to go in?" And before you know it, the big snake slithers around the wall and hisses at you angrily. Now you can see his size: He is tremendous! His head is as big as a good-sized living room, and his fangs are like large tusks. He appears very fierce and belligerent.

He repeats again, "Do you really want to go in?"

Well, with this kind of welcoming committee, very few people would be encouraged to enter and most would have second thoughts about it. You say to the snake, "Will you open your mouth a little wider, please?"

He is clearly caught by surprise, and certainly has not been expecting this response to his hissing and carrying on. So he opens his mouth wider, and you can already see his big throat. Then you say, "Open just a bit more, please."

The snake looks puzzled. He stops hissing and is, obviously, at a loss about what to expect next. But he goes along and opens his mouth really wide. At this point, you jump right down his throat and keep going. Now comes a long trip through the snake's belly, and lo, you emerge into the light of Nirvana from the other end of the snake. (Even the guardian of Nirvana, like all other snakes, has two ends.)

Well, you did it. It is not the most dignified way to enter Nirvana, nor is it a very legal one, but you are in. You leave the snake behind to ponder the consequences of all that happened and go about exploring Nirvana, before he gets around to doing something about your illegal entry.

It is really a nice place. What a contrast to the dark void outside! It's difficult to describe the good "vibes" and the all-pervading light. As you move along, you find high thronelike structures, all luminous, with people sitting cross-legged on them, meditating. Some angels are hanging over them, apparently for decoration. Bliss pervades everything. The people are totally unaware of what is happening around them, for they are immersed in their meditation, experiencing constant and intense bliss.

Upon closer examination, you find that this state of bliss is caused by pure consciousness—the void flowing through their bodies. It enters their heads and flows down and out the bottoms of their spines. From there it flows into the Manifest

Creation, which is located below them. You are able to examine the heads of these people, and find, to your surprise, that they contain no thoughts. The thinking process would interfere with and alter the flow of pure consciousness. These beings are drawing the flow of consciousness through them, but are not affecting it in any way.

Seeing all these pure and exalted beings, you begin to feel remorseful about the trick you pulled on the snake. Not wanting him to get into trouble with the authorities because of your illegal behavior, you go back to the cashier's window to apologize. The snake—let us call him Naga—turns out to be a good sport. "Well," he says cheerfully, "win a few, lose a few; you can't win them all. It was a neat trick you pulled on me." Encouraged by Naga's attitude, you start asking him about his work and about Nirvana in general.

"Nirvana, as you know," he says, "is really a blind alley of evolution. People are interested solely in their own bliss, and they don't care about others. That's why I'm supposed to scare them away from here. But if they decide to come in anyway, in spite of my warnings, it's their right. They worked for it and are entitled to their bliss. However, they will not evolve beyond this."

Emboldened by Naga's friendly behavior, you ask him for a guided tour of Nirvana. "I guess I can take off," he says, "business is slow today." And with that, he flips out his enormous forked tongue, picks you up, deposits you on his back, and off you go. Naga slithers rapidly among the thrones, making some snide remarks here and there. You notice that the people in Nirvana are practically all Easterners. "Yes," says Naga, "the West has not discovered it yet. And besides, Westerners seem more active and tend not to come here."

You find that by whispering sweet little things into Naga's ear, and especially by scratching him behind his ear, you can make him quite talkative and downright humorous. He has a good, dry humor. "Traffic has been very slow here in the last few millennia, and it's getting worse. Nowadays people care more for each other, and wanting to help the evolution of their fellow men, they bypass Nirvana. We are considering closing down the place or operating with only a skeleton crew," Naga points at his protruding ribs with a sigh.

Soon we are back at his post near the window. You say goodbye to your new friend, scratch him behind the ear once more, kiss him on the nose, and off you go, back into the void.

The Blue-Collar Workers

It occurs to you that if most of the traffic of enlightened souls is not into Nirvana nowadays, then there must be a better place for them to go, and you set out to look for it.

It doesn't take long before you run into a group of people sitting cross-legged in the dark. As you take a closer look you see that one fellow is much taller than the others. He seems to be the Buddha. You slowly recognize the other people as famous yogis, who have departed a long time ago from the physical level; there are also some more recent arrivals. They all seem to be sitting cross-legged, except for one figure, resembling St. Augustine, who is walking around with a cross as if it were a placard. He looks as if he is picketing the place.

Upon closer scrutiny, you find that these people are every bit as developed as the population in Nirvana—even more so. Pure consciousness flows through their bodies, entering through their heads, where again no thought process is visible, and emerging from the bottom of their spines. From there it flows into the Manifest Creation. The difference is that these people tamper a little with the void as it flows through them. They are adding a slight vibration to it, prebiasing the flow of consciousness, in order to produce a certain effect on the evolution of their particular planets.

You may recall from the previous chapter how tendencies are imparted on the flow of pure consciousness by the layers of letters at the outer boundary of Manifest Creation. One group of "Blue-Collar Workers" is adding an extra twist and direction to the tendencies imparted to the void by the layers of letters.

72

We have here, then, a group of people whose compassion makes them work hard for the evolution of beings on their respective planets. They are, in effect, a planetary lobby, doing a twenty-four-hour-a-day job day in, day out. They have renounced the option of eternal bliss in Nirvana, and instead sit in the dark void, doing thankless jobs. But, as we all know, this kind of selfless work eventually pays off. They will keep evolving, and in time leave the population of Nirvana far behind.

The Zoo

You have made yourself familiar with two groups of advanced beings and are ready to explore some more of this interesting and lively void.

You push on into the darkness. After a while, some light becomes visible far away, and you go there. Again, you find a wall with a barred window. You go nearer and look in. What a surprise: a whole zoo of animals! There is a tiger, an elephant, a monkey, a goat or some antelopelike animal, and a dog, all of them sitting in this enclosure. You are very puzzled. A zoo

ABSOLUTE ZOO

in the Absolute? Why a *zoo*? Then the answer comes. Something is explaining that this is only a mental image to symbolize how we human beings embody in various degrees the traits that these animals represent. In other words, there is some of the aggressive predator in us, the wisdom and strength of the elephant, the frivolousness of the chattering monkey, the steadiness of the goat, and the faithfulness of the dog.

Again you have learned something useful. You acknowledge that this is all very interesting and at the same time realize that your thinking process has changed. You assumed that once you reached the Absolute, the thinking processes would automatically come to a stop. But here you go, romping around in the void and apparently thinking. This present thinking process is not the kind of linear, deductive thinking that people normally do, but rather an intuitive knowing, where very complex ideas are imprinted on the mind instantaneously.

Some questions are still nagging you. Why is there such lively activity in the Absolute? What or who is the something that explains things to you out here, in the void? And, finally, who is running the show?

The Absolute Paradox

In our lives there are always two states, the "real" and the "ideal." The real is the Manifest Creation, of which we are a part, and the ideal is what we bring to life in our minds. In our physical state, the real, we travel in our mind to the ideal, or we could say that Manifest Creation keeps expanding to reach the Absolute. However, by the time we catch up with the ideal, the mind has already moved ahead to a new ideal.

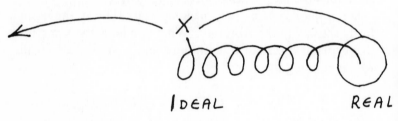

IDEAL   REAL

So you are always chasing yourself. Your ideal is never within your Creation, but attached to it and running ahead of it, like a carrot in front of a mule. Nirvana, the Blue-Collar-Workers,

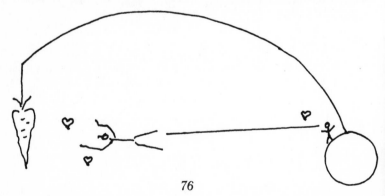

and the zoo appear to be in the Absolute, because they are a mind state, a potential, and they become real the minute you achieve that state. That is, in an expanded state of consciousness you can experience them as real.

The vision of the ideal is always outside the Creation and precedes it. The vision pulls the Creation along. Here are the dynamics of it: The carrot (the ideal) extends from Creation on a string. As Creation expands, it moves, and so does the carrot. You reach out for the carrot, never realizing it is attached and part of your own Creation. In a sense, Nirvana (or any ideal) is also Creation, only in the mind. In other words, you can eat the carrot, but only in your dreams.

Or, to put it another way, it is like having a dream in which you have just won a lottery and are about to get the money when you wake up. That is the whole story in a nutshell. You keep on living to win the lottery, and you keep winning it, but only in your dreams, so that you never have the money in your pocket. You can not take Nirvana to the bank. But from the viewpoint of the dream or mind state, maybe the physical is unreal? You may not be able to take Nirvana to the bank, but who says the bank is real? It can all be reversed and you could say that it is the Manifest Creation pulling the Absolute along, rather than the Absolute pushing the Creation. Each wants to be where the other is, but they can never come together. In essence, however, they are one and the same, the Manifest Creation being the Absolute itself projected into form from its potential state.

We can visualize it as two balls: one, the Absolute, containing the ideal (Nirvana and all the rest), and the other a satellite ball, the Manifest Creation. Your perception of reality depends on where you stand. Whichever side you are on always appears to be the positive or true reality. Each side sees the other as negative, unreal, or potential. The real, what is yours, is always what you hold in your hand.

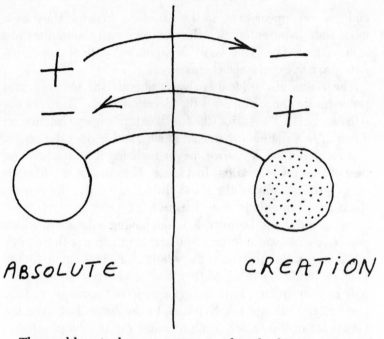

The problem is that we are too used to thinking in terms of things being absolutely positive or negative, forgetting that what is over there is positive to itself, and what is here is negative to it. Positive and negative are as relative as *here* and *there*, and even the Absolute is relative in this sense. The Manifest Creation is where you stand; the Absolute is where you don't stand. To illustrate, suppose you die and according to your level of consciousness find yourself in Nirvana. Then Nirvana becomes your reality, your Manifest Creation, and the physical reality, which you have left behind, becomes your potential. The individualized consciousness is a part of the reality in which it finds itself.

There is nothing absolute and final. If everything were iron-clad, all the rules absolute and everything structured so no paradox or irony existed, you couldn't move. One could say that man sneaks through the crack where paradox exists.

Part 5

WHO'S RUNNING THE SHOW?

Meeting Your Higher Self

Until now, whenever you dealt with a structure, you knew that it was a being who was therefore relatively easy to contact. Now you are in a place where there is no more structure. You are out in the infinite void or Absolute. Who is the boss here? Is it possible that He is giving you this guided tour? There must be someone minding the store. It's just too big a place to be without a boss. Who is running the show?

You decide to call on the being responsible for All-there-is. So you stick out your chest and say in a challenging voice, "I want to see the top God. Who is in charge here, anyway?"

Suddenly, a great column of blinding light appears in front of you. The light is so powerful, and the vibrations emanating from the column so overwhelming, that for a moment you feel like the sorcerer's apprentice. You bit off more than you can chew. Your teeth are rattling, your knees are a little wobbly. It takes you a while to get used to this powerful, radiant presence.

Since it is impossible to see into this column because of its blinding brilliance, and you don't want to miss the opportunity to meet the real boss of the system, you have to devise some ingenious way of solving the problem, just as with the Naga before. You notice that the bottom of the column of light is open. It's like a tube or skirt, and the light emanating from it is not as powerful. Well, you figure, if you could only peek under this skirt, you would certainly see something, if not the entirety, of that being. This idea appears very irreverent, but certainly workable. With some trepidation, you peek under

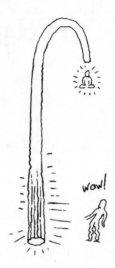

the rim of this column of light, and to your great surprise find
that it is just a hollow tube. It's a tall tunnel of light, disappear-
ing far up in the distance.

"Well," you think to yourself, "a tunnel is an invitation to
enter." So, up the tube you go. And you go, and go. After a
while you feel that the tube is bending for some reason; it's
bending some more, and more, and you feel that you have
made a U-turn. Now you are moving downward very rapidly.
Soon you have lost control and are hurtling down the tube.

Suddenly, you see the end of the tube, and something is
sitting there. You realize that the something you see must be
IT, the real thing! You are scared and all this is happening very
fast now. You pop out of the tube and there, in front of you sits
. . . the Lord of the system. He sits cross-legged—and guess
who it is? It is *yourself!* It is your SELF. It's a carbon copy of
your physical body, completely immobile, calm, unperturbed,
and impersonal. This, certainly, is quite a surprise. You try to
pull yourself together: Okay, what do you say to yourself?

He does not look at you; his eyes are focused in the distance. And there you are, finding yourself in an awkward situation. You came a long and arduous way to find the answers to your quest, and there it sits: Yourself. It's unbelievable, but there sits your SELF.

Since verbal communication makes little sense here, you decide to use the old tested merging technique, which you used when you had to find out what the different beings and gods you ran into were all about. You turn around and start backing slowly into your body. This is done very carefully, just

like trying to back a car into a very tight garage. You are almost merged with your body, when suddenly you just click into it, and—BANG! The whole thing explodes! There are no bodies, just the void. You have become the void. You *are* the void.

It takes a while to get oriented in this new situation. But it is quite clear now that the SELF is the void. You have been the void all along. You are pure consciousness or pure awareness, and that is the supreme SELF that has been guiding you through the long and eventful trip back to *itself*. This was the observer looking through the pupils of your eyes over hundreds or thousands of lifetimes, making sense of your experiences. That pure awareness, which is the void, gave you your awareness of self, or self-awareness.

So, *you* are the Supreme God of the system! At the same time you are the person doing a nine-to-five job, pushing a pencil or driving a truck, paying income tax and phone bills. And not only are you this Supreme God, but so is everybody else. We are all part of pure consciousness, the void. The consciousness breaks down into units, and each has an awareness of self and thinks that he is different from everybody else.

Summing It Up

The home of the Supreme SELF is the Absolute, the void. Then after a long time, this SELF, sitting in the cold, dark void, gets bored and wants to do something. Being creative, He wants to play, since there is no work to be done out there. (He does not need to earn a living.) He finds no company and, therefore, starts playing with Himself.

He decides to play hide-and-seek, because it's an easy game to play. He quickly manifests a blanket made of ego-stuff (in the Absolute everything is possible.) Then He separates a part of Himself and covers it with this blanket of ego, and goes "Boo!" Well, this is a very interesting and delightful game. So, He gets another blanket of ignorance of Self and wraps it around the previous blanket. This looks like fun, he thinks, and adds a blanket of intellect and of emotion, more ignorance, and a thick physical blanket.

Soon the part that is all wrapped up in ignorance and ego stops recognizing the original SELF. He is so involved in the goings-on inside His cocoon of blankets that He completely ignores and forgets His playful part. He is now down to the physical level of consciousness, the so-called physical reality. Unaware of him*self*, He is like the king, so the tale goes, who put on rags and went out among the people, to find out what real life is all about. Unfortunately, the king became so involved in real life, he forgot about being a king. It seems that it took quite a few traumas to remind him of his real status.

And so it goes with us. We are so deeply immersed in this rat race of ours that we have all but forgotten our real status. But the SELF in the void has not. He is still playing. Now and then He will lift the blankets and say, "Hi, there!" but most of the time, we are too busy to notice Him. However, He won't let go, and we will get another stimulus, and another, until we start responding. The SELF will be pleased. He will continue to stimulate us.

Suddenly we develop strange feelings of inadequacy. Something is missing from our life. Is this nine-to-five job really all I want to do with my life? Isn't there something more to it? And so we start searching. We look to the West and we look to the East. We look into religions and cults. Sooner or later things crystallize, and we step on the path of spiritual development.

The SELF likes that and keeps tickling us under the blankets. Sooner or later, one blanket of ignorance drops, then

another, and another. We start receiving intuitive knowledge about the system. The trip becomes more and more exhilarating. Now the SELF is really happy, as He watches the process unfold. Finally, the last blanket has come off, and we are facing the SELF at the end of the tube. "Welcome," says the SELF, "welcome home." And you look at Him and say, "And who are you?" "Well," says the SELF, "I am you! Don't you remember, silly? Just a few eons ago we were one and the same. We started playing hide-and-seek, and you got all wrapped up in your blankets and lost sight of me. But I kept watching you all along."

Then a glimmer of ancient memories starts coming back to you. You realize that *He* is *you* and *you* are *He*. So, you hug your SELF—the quest has ended. Now you know that you are the SELF, the Supreme God of this system. You also know that you contain the infinite void and it contains you. In short, you are IT! Self-realization has occurred.

Happy ending.

Just so that you won't think that I have invented all this only for your amusement, I would like to quote from the writings of a wise old Indian sage, Shankara, who lived about twelve centuries ago. Here is what he says about this:

> *On the vast canvas of the Self*
> *the picture of the manifold worlds*
> *is painted by the Self itself.*
> *And that Supreme Self,*
> *seeing but itself,*
> *enjoys great delight.*

THE END
And the beginning . . .

APPENDIX

What is a Hologram?

Holography is one of the key concepts in this new paradigm; yet, many people have difficulty understanding what holograms are and how they work. Here is a simple analogy of how nature stores information holographically.

Imagine you have a shallow pan of water into which three pebbles are dropped simultaneously. Each pebble is the source of waves spreading evenly across the pan. The waves cross and interact with one another, creating a complex pattern called an *interference pattern*. If you now quick-freeze the surface of the water in the pan and lift out the resulting rippled sheet of ice, you are then holding a record of the interference pattern of the waves. This is a hologram.

If you illuminate the sheet of ice with a coherent light source (light of the same frequency, in which all waves are "in step"— e.g., a laser) and then look through the air toward the light,

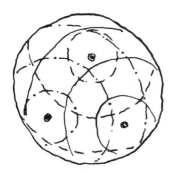

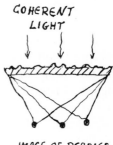

COHERENT LIGHT

IMAGE OF PEBBLES

you will see an image of the three pebbles suspended in mid-air, and they look three-dimensional! The rippled ice surface acts as a distorted lens in such a way as to focus the light to points taken up by the pebbles that have caused the ripples. The chaotic-looking ice surface is actually a holographic information storage device. Amazingly, if you take the sheet of ice and break it into small pieces, and illuminate one of the chips, you will again see the image of all three pebbles projected in midair, just as each cell in our bodies carries all of the genetic information necessary to make an additional exact copy of our bodies. Holography is nature's most compact information storage device.

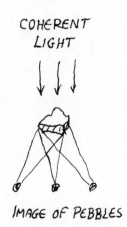

COHERENT LIGHT

IMAGE OF PEBBLES

Holography is actually a method of lensless photography in which the wave field of light scattered by an object—an apple, say—is recorded as an interference pattern. A laser light beam is split into two components by a half-mirror. This allows part of the beam to continue undisturbed while part of it is deflected to another mirror. Both narrow beams are spread open by lenses. The undisturbed beam, called the *reference beam*, arrives at a photographic plate after an eventless flight, and deposits its imprint on the film. The deflected beam, called

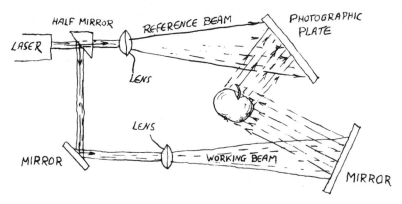

the *working beam,* encounters the object and then is reflected onto the film. In a sense, the working beam tells the reference beam about its experiences with the object by creating an interference pattern on the film that stores information about the object. Information can be elicited from the film by illuminating it with the same laser light used in making the hologram. As we do that, we see the apple appear suspended in midair, looking very three-dimensional and real. And because holograms have the property of *total distributedness,* illuminating any piece of the original hologram will produce the *entire* image of the apple.

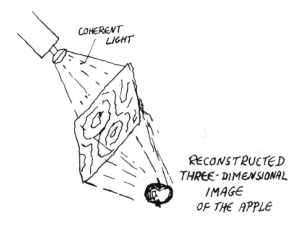

The important part of making a holographic image is the interaction of the *reference beam*—a beam that is pure and untouched—with a *working beam,* a beam that has had some experiences. The magnitude of these experiences is measured against the reference beam, which serves as a baseline for comparison.

Our daily reality is constructed by constantly making such comparisons. Our senses, which describe our reality to us, are making these comparisons all the time (e.g., relative hot and cold). But the senses do not have any absolute reference line, only relative reference beams for relative comparisons.

However, our psyches form an interference pattern with all other units of consciousness in the universe. This Universal Mind hologram, or the Absolute, contains all frequencies, and each level of consciousness can relate to it as its *absolute reference beam.*

The implications of this holographic model are monumental. It implies that all the knowledge in the Universal Mind is available to anyone who can tune into it, because, as in all holograms, the information is totally distributed throughout the universe. Mystical aphorisms such as "We are all one," "As above, so below," "God is within you," and "The universe in a grain of sand" take on a new meaning when seen in the light of the holographic model.*

* Reprinted courtesy of *New Age* magazine, September 1977. By I. Bentov.

If we draw a line and place dots on it representing individual consciousnesses, and from each dot draw diverging lines, representing expanding consciousness, we see that the higher the level, the more areas overlap. On the highest spiritual level, they will all blend onto one, showing that on that level the consciousness of mankind is one.

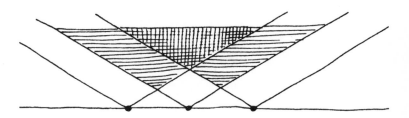

So here we are—all part of this great hologram called Creation, which is everybody else's SELF. You can't blame anybody for doing anything to you—you are doing it to yourself. You create your own reality. It's all a cosmic play, and there is nothing but *you!*

Essay On Cosmology
by Edward Apgar

Once in a great while a human soul appears on the earthly scene with a passionate curiosity directed at all realms of experience, free of inhibitions, which cause so many to fragment and compartmentalize their interests. All too often, we prefer the security of a few special areas and profess bafflement at all others. Contrast this with the outlook of Leonardo da Vinci, Isaac Newton, and, more recently, the polymathematician John von Neumann. They (and others less well known) manage to retain their childhood vitality of vision and see the world as a single, untangled web, in which all parts are connected in a grand pattern.

Itzhak Bentov definitely belongs in this category of "wholistic perceivers." In this book and his earlier one, *Stalking the Wild Pendulum*, Bentov's insights range from the evolution of consciousness and the mechanics of meditation to the large-scale structure of the universe.

Although his cosmological model is quite worthy of standing alone as a description of physical reality, subject to comparison with factual observations and new discoveries, one point should be emphasized at the start of such an examination: Itzhak Bentov's primary interest was *knowledge of the self* as the route to ultimate knowledge in all areas. His cosmology came almost as a by-product of his lifetime search for self-knowledge and his studies of the higher harmonics of physical reality.

This distinction is important in view of the many recent publications on the relationship between modern science and Eastern mysticism. Bentov's viewpoint is distinctly different from that of other writers who stress the fascinating analogies between physics and mysticism (such as Lawrence LeShan), or those who describe an apparent convergence of mysticism and modern physics (such as Fritjof Capra).

The Bentov cosmology is the opposite of the standard reductionist attempts to construct a model of consciousness based on ingenious mechanisms of such disciplines as chemistry, electricity, and quantum theory.

Bentov, whose cosmology was a by-product of his personal spiritual insights and mystical visions, was able to access deep intuitive sources of images and sketch out a view of "how things are." He used physical explanations and models as aids and metaphors to give scientifically literate readers a better appreciation of his visions.

In his writing and teaching, Bentov expressed in vivid terms an age-old feeling of connection between our inner experiences and the large-scale phenomena of the surrounding universe.

For a few million years and through thousands of generations of evolution, humanity has been on earth, looking with wonder at the oceans, mountains, and stars. The surviving folklore of the native American Indians provides powerful examples of this. One can imagine that states of expanded awareness, stimulated by exposure to the vastness of natural phenomena, have a genetic origin that is due to this long-term racial "memory." Coupled with such states is usually the urge to understand the structure and the origin of the cosmos, which would bring the seeds of answers to equally burning questions about human origins and our ultimate destiny.

Attempts to understand cosmic processes beyond the limits

of everyday experience must necessarily stretch everyday modes of perception to a breaking point and make us receptive to new ways of viewing reality.

There are examples of how the creative giants of science were inspired by feeling of awe, mystery, wonder, and search for beauty. Pythagoras, Archimedes, Copernicus, Galileo, Kepler, Newton, Maxwell, and Einstein readily come to mind. Their creative impulse could not be confined to one narrow public domain to satisfy their psychological and spiritual quest for meaning. Einstein, as usual, had the appropriate remark. "Religion without science is lame and science without religion is blind."

Although Bentov saw farther than most in the spiritual dimension, his feet were firmly on the ground of the contemporary world of science. He was a product of his times, and by a curious coincidence, his lifespan parallelled almost exactly the development of modern cosmology.

Hints of an expanding universe were contained in Einstein's general theory of relativity and puzzled over in 1917, but it was not until the early 1920s that evidence for a general expansion of the universe began to be taken seriously, with the postulation of the "red-shift."

In the explosion of information from advances in the many special fields of science, it is easy to look upon cosmology as just one of many equally important special studies. The amazing fact is that in spite of being one of the most rapidly advancing and exciting fields, along with particle physics, to which it is closely related, cosmology, with its subdivision astronomy, is the oldest science. Its origins go back to the time before the origins of the scientific method, when folklore and mythology were the forms of explanation of reality.

In modern terms, cosmology is the study of the origins, structure, and properties of the entire universe, such as the distribution of galaxies and the density and motion of matter and energy, visible and invisible. It has developed rapidly as a science only in the last sixty years, with the invention of sophisticated instrumentation. Prior to this, astronomers concentrated primarily on the study of the planets and the comparatively few stars visible to the naked eye.

However, even before the invention of the telescope, the observations of Copernicus, Brahe, and Kepler in the sixteenth century triggered a revolution in thought, which, like the first of a row of dominoes, led to the scientific revolution and the successive developments of modern technology. This initial revolution consisted of a simple change in perspective— from the earth-centered universe of Ptolemy to the sun-centered solar system of Copernicus, later refined and perfected by Galileo and Newton. This breakthrough from ancient to modern thought, supported by evidence that could be understood by the person in the street, made it permissible, even respectable, to question all old habits of thought and dicta of authorities.

In the eighteenth century there followed, in rapid succession, new ideas in chemistry, biology, and physiology, such as the emergence of genetics as a new science and the discovery of the phenomenon of the circulation of blood. In the nineteenth century, Darwin's theory of evolution and the principle of natural selection were followed by the first great unification theory in physics, namely, Maxwell's theory of electricity and magnetism. The culmination of this outburst of creativity was Einstein's special theory of relativity at the threshold of the twentieth century.

The latter development was unique in being the first scientific advance to undermine the mechanistic tradition of an objective reality and the absolute meaning attached to the concepts of space, time, and simultaneity. Einstein proved that these had meaning only in connection with the choice of observer, reference system, and means of measurement, i.e., the clock and the light beam.

Later, quantum theory, as expressed by Bohr and Heisenberg, would go even further in questioning the reality of a permanent, objective world beyond the observer. What this shows is that new insights into the nature of the surrounding universe are not merely the spin-off of a special scientific viewpoint, rather, the way we see the world affects our habits of thought in all areas.

Rapid successive developments in science during the last four hundred years were only the prelude to the revolutionary developments in cosmology, which took place between 1916 and 1925. In the space of a few years, "common-sense" notions were shaken by indications that the universe was far larger, older, and more complex than had ever been dreamed of previously. In fact, it seemed to be blowing up before our eyes! Attempts to explain these observations brought an outburst of new theories and models of the universe, culminating fifty years later in Itzhak Bentov's model of the "modest continuous bang" universe.

Surrounded as we are by mass media presentations of exciting new discoveries on a regular basis, we may not fully appreciate how radical a change in view took place in the early part of this century. For thousands of years, the universe was seen as little more than the earth, the sun, the planets, and the surrounding stars, with no apparent structure except for the band of stars called the Milky Way.

In the early 1700s, shortly after the telescope was first pointed at the heavens, two nonprofessionals, Thomas Wright and the philosopher Emmanuel Kant, speculated that certain fuzzy nebulosities might be, instead of stars, far-off galaxies similar to our own Milky Way.

The most prominent "fuzzy spot" was the Great Nebula in Andromeda, studied for centuries by the naked eye. Experts disagreed as to whether it was part of our Milky Way galaxy. Then William Herschel, a self-taught amateur astronomer, observed hundreds of similar fuzzy formations. Still, most experts, including Harlow Shapley, the most outspoken advocate of the single galaxy view, denied the existence of anything beyond the limits of our own galaxy.

Building on the pioneering work of Henrietta Leavitt on Cepheid variables, Shapley mapped the size and structure of the Milky Way for the first time. In the face of increasing contrary evidence, he insisted that it was unique and, in effect, represented the entire universe! However, as a result of a famous debate in 1920 between Shapley and another astronomer, Heber Curtis, evidence for the existence of "outside" galaxies gained acceptance, and the new view of the universe as larger and more complex began to grow. This trend has continued to the present day with the discovery of radio sources, quasars, pulsars, and "bubble" formations, as well as with theoretical suggestions of black holes, strings, and so on.

The other exciting cosmological discovery of the twentieth century was the idea of an expanding universe. The first clues came from the work of V. M. Slipher, who, between 1912 and 1925, studied the optical spectra of more than twenty galaxies. He found a pattern in which well-known stellar spectral lines were shifted toward the longer red wavelengths of the spectrum, compared with the same lines seen in nearby and earthly environments. Using the Doppler effect, the observation suggested that the stars and the galaxies, which are the sources of these "red-shifted" spectral lines, are rapidly receding from the observers on earth.

This interpretation of the red-shift, and the discovery that the universe is a collection of galaxies, gave birth to the radical new idea of rapid expansion of the universe in all directions. The exact proportionality between the amount of the red-shift and the distance to the corresponding galaxies and stars, as determined by other methods, is known as Hubble's Law, after its discoverer, Edwin Hubble, who devoted thirty years to detailed studies of the expansion of the universe. Extrapolation backwards in time suggests that the universe began its expansion between 10 and 20 billion years ago.

Theoreticians were not far behind the experimentalists in producing new descriptions of the universe. Ten years after publishing his special theory of relativity, Albert Einstein created the general theory of relativity, which contained the amazing assertion that the classical geometry of Euclid was not strictly accurate in the vicinity of large masses! In fact, Einstein showed that gravitation is not a simple force but an indication of curvature in a four-dimensional "space-time" manifold.

When applied to the universe, this new theory seemed to predict an instability: that the universe is not static but is expanding in all directions from any chosen point of reference.

In 1916 this idea was considered too radical. The red-shift results were not well known. To compensate, Einstein added an extra term, the "cosmological constant," which canceled the expansion effect. However, other theoreticians, such as Alexander Friedmann and Abbé Lemaître, did similar calculations with Einstein's equations and took the predicted expansion seriously. Lemaître even suggested that the universe began with the explosion of a "primeval atom" or "cosmic egg." However, the pace of discovery during the few years from 1916 to 1930 was so rapid that it took more time for the scientific establishment to digest the new ideas. Consequently, for a few decades, only a small group of pioneer cosmologists continued to work in relative isolation.

For example, in 1939 J. R. Oppenheimer published a prediction of the existence of a "black hole," which no one took seriously for many years. Also, the idea of the universe originating in a "big bang" explosion was ignored as an academic exercise, until George Gamov, years later showed how, with the aid of this concept, one could predict the existence and abundance of elements in the universe.

Let us stop and look back over this dizzy journey of "self-discovery," in a physical sense, on which humanity has traveled during these last few turbulent decades. After resting comfortably for thousands of years with the idea of the universe as a group of planets, a sun, and a surrounding cloud of stars in a stable, enduring configuration, suddenly in almost an eye's blink, civilization had to adjust to the radical view that we live on a minor planet in a galaxy of 10^{11} stars, itself only one in an exploding universe of 10^{11} galaxies! Suddenly, we see the universe in a new light. It has a beginning, a possible end, a specific size, structure, and shape!

As time went on, difficulties impeded the acceptance of the big bang cosmology. First, there was a problem with explaining the formation of heavy elements in the rapid initial expansion, later explained by Fred Hoyle as originating in the interior of stars and dispersed in supernova explosions. This means that most of the objects around us, including the elements in our bodies, were once in the interior of a star!

The other difficulty was of time scale. Early estimates on the age of the universe as being about 1.8 billion years were in obvious conflict with earthly, 5-billion-year-old rocks. This was eventually corrected to approximately 15 billion when more accurate values of the size of the universe and Hubble's constant were obtained.

During this period of debate and consolidation, some alternate cosmologies were advocated. Many scientists felt uncomfortable with the big bang model, in spite of the red-shift evidence in its favor. It raised many new questions: "What existed before the explosion?" "Where did the matter and energy come from?" "Will the universe keep expanding forever and eventually just fade away, or will it collapse back on itself and destroy everything?"

As an alternative to these perplexing questions, astrophysicists Thomas Gold, Herman Bondi, and Fred Hoyle proposed, about 1950, a steady-state model of the universe. In this model, new matter is continually created to match the rate of expansion described by Hubble's measurements. There is no need for a specific beginning or for an eventual end. New galaxies and stars keep forming to fill in the spaces left by expansion. For this scheme to work, it is only necessary for some mechanism to create one hydrogen atom per year in a volume the size of a modern skyscraper building, obviously too small a quantity to measure directly.

This model also had difficulties. One problem came from the discovery of quasi-stellar objects, or "QSO" for convenience. These QSO include quasi-stellar radio sources, or "quasars," and nonradio quasi-stellar objects. The optical spectra of QSO give red-shift values many times greater than those of ordinary galaxies. If one assumes that QSO distances are related to recession velocities in the same way as ordinary galaxies, then their large red-shift values indicate that they are at immense distances. However, the apparent brightness of QSO is such that if they are at great distances, their intrinsic brightness may be up to one hundred times that of the brightest ordinary galaxies. Most QSO fit this picture and seem to have been created shortly after the "big bang," although a few exceptions have been recently discovered. Thus, the universe is not in a steady-state equilibrium. Something unique happened 10 to 15 billion years ago.

A serious blow to Hoyle's continuous creation theory was the discovery of the background radio "noise," uniform in all directions, with a temperature of three degrees Kelvin. This was predicted by the big bang theorists, especially George Gamov, but not taken seriously for many years, until its accidental discovery by two radio engineers at the Bell laboratories. This radiation was interpreted as the primordial energy left over from the big bang explosion, and, following this triumphant verification, the big bang model has remained the accepted theory of the creation of the universe.

Until recently, the general absence of observations of galaxies forming supported the continuous creation or steady-state theory. However, in 1983, the infrared orbiting telescope IRAS brought new data about stars and galaxies that previously were invisible using optical means. To the astronomers' surprise, innumerable stars were discovered at different stages of development.

This evidence was recently expanded by the discovery of a galaxy in its initial stages of formation, a "proto-galaxy." A report from the January 1987 meeting of the American Astronomical Society describes a galaxy observed today as it was 12 billion years ago, owing to its distance, when the universe was about 4 billion years old and believed to be past its epoch of galaxy formation. This discovery suggests that the epoch must have lasted longer than was previously believed.

Interestingly enough, this evidence of the continuation of the process of creation of new stars and galaxies reflects the "continuous bang" of the evolving stream of energy-matter of the Bentov model.

There are many additional contributions to the history of cosmology, which we cannot explore in detail. P. A. M. Dirac has suggested a cosmology in which matter is created near existing matter, and, with a variable gravitational constant, G. H. Arp and others have questioned the validity of the Hubble red-shift relation to QSO, and suggested non-Doppler sources of red-shift. If this turns out to be true, the universe could be smaller and younger than is thought at present.

This survey indicates that the evolution of cosmological thought has not been smooth and predictable. Ideas now accepted as commonplace were sometimes considered strange and unacceptable when first proposed. We are now in a better position to appreciate Bentov's model and to see its novel aspects.

The Bentov model of the universe, if one could see it from "outside," would appear as an elongated torus, like a melon, with funnel-like cavities at each end, as shown in the diagram on page 14. At the center of the torus, which is constantly turning itself inside out like a smoke ring, there is a white and a black hole back to back.

The process of creation is a continuous fountain of pure energy emerging from the white hole as a jet flowing along the axis of one of the funnels, which we will call, for convenience, the "north" end of the axis. As the jet expands, it cools and condenses to form particles, such as electrons, protons, and neutrons, as well as photons, which remain in space as primordial background radiation.

As these particles stream away from the source, they continue to cool and collect into clouds of helium and hydrogen gas, which then condense under gravitational forces into galaxies and stars. Within the stars heavy elements are formed, which in turn form planetary systems. As this massive jet further expands and slows down, gravity continues to act and to cause it to bend and spread in all directions, away from the axis of symmetry of the north funnel. It continues to curve away, until it eventually bends around completely, falling like a cosmic fountain, back toward its origin. Eventually, this spread-out jet undergoes a gravitational collapse into the other funnel, at the south end of the melon-shaped torus, and is pulled back into the focal region by the gravitation of the black hole. There it is transmuted into pure energy and reemerges from the white hole as a "new" universe.

If we shift from this external viewpoint to that of an observer inside the torus on some planet orbiting a star in a galaxy, an entirely different viewpoint exists. Such an observer would see, in all directions, stars and galaxies in apparent recession, as if partaking in a big bang process. As the observer's local region of the jet stream moves further and further away from the focal point in the torus, it expands to a maximum size, and then begins to collapse back to greater density as it is drawn into the black hole.

This is, in a brief nonquantitative form, an outline of Bentov's modest continuous bang model of the universe. We see that it has the unique feature of combining the apparently contradictory theories of the big bang and the steady-state. *The observations depend on the viewpoint of the observer,* since we are on the "inside," we interpret the data as indicating a discontinuous big bang process at work, whereas if observed from the "outside," it can be seen as a continuous process.

Such seeming contradictions are not a new situation in physics. We remember the wave-particle duality, in which the so-called "facts" about the nature of light depend on the choice of the observing equipment. If the experimenter directs the light at a system of narrow slits, diffraction effects, indicative of waves, are seen. If, instead of slits, particle detectors are used, discrete photons with specific locations are measured. Light is neither a wave nor a particle. It displays dual attributes, which depend on the method of observation.

In a similar way, the big bang is reality for an observer inside the Bentov universe, while an observer who is able to move "outside" the universe into a higher dimension, physically or in an expanded state of consciousness, as was the case with Bentov, would see a modest continuous bang structure, in which there is no beginning and no end to creation. Thus, the universe is finite or infinite, depending on one's state of observation!

Bentov's own words from his letter of March 13, 1968, to the astrophysicist Fred Hoyle summarize this idea: "This model tries to show that the two major ideas prevailing in cosmology today—the steady-state and the big bang theories—are not really contradicting each other, but are complementary and exist simultaneously."

It is difficult to point to any simple quantitative confirmation of Bentov's model. Consider that it took more than thirty years of intensive research to distinguish between the alternate theories of Hubble and Hoyle. If the size of the cosmic torus is large in comparison with that of the observer's visible sphere of galaxies, then no decisive calculations would appear possible. With a smaller torus or with the use of more sensitive telescopes, some useful data might be detected.

An early example of such data is the observation of a small anisotropy (or unevenness) in the distribution of quasars in the north and south poles of the observable sky. On the basis of this fact, Bentov placed our galaxy at the point of expansion of the jet, because the density of the quasars in the north galactic pole would be less than that in the south, where the observer from the earth would be looking back into the source of the jet.

Again, in Bentov's 1968 letter to Hoyle:

> . . . then it makes sense to expect fewer fast quasars in the northern hemisphere because of their age, loss of energy, and possible evolution into radio galaxies. This will explain also the ratio between the number of slow and fast quasars. On the other hand, the southern hemisphere, which is the source of the quasars, should have more fast ones, and the numerical ratio between the fast and the slow quasars should be smaller . . . we find the cones of vision for the fast vs. the slow quasars agreeing fairly well with the distribution data in the book, *Quasi-Stellar Objects*, Burbridge & Burbridge, 1967.

More recent quasar data might permit a better judgment of the validity of the Bentov model. Quasars, the radio emission variety of QSO, play an important part in Bentov's thinking. He was struck by the photograph of a QSO displaying a structure of a dense central core ejecting a jet of matter into space for hundreds or thousands of light years. He discusses several such quasars in his 1968 letter, especially the ones designated 3C273 and 3C275.1, and uses this jet mechanism as a supportive analogy to his torus model of the universe, with its close association between a white hole jet source and a black hole sink. To emphasize this analogy, he called quasars a "chip off the old block."

Another recent possible confirmation of the model is an observation of a streaming effect of local matter, relative to the isotropic background radiation. In the *New York Times* of December 2, 1986, evidence is presented for the jet-like movement of galaxies:

> This galaxy and its thousands of neighbors in a gigantic portion of the universe appear to be streaming across at speeds of more than 400 miles per second. . . . The report of this vast celestial convoy has caused growing excitement, bewilderment and some disbelief in astrophysics circles since the first word of their findings. Of the many competing theories for the formation of structure in the universe, none predicted this "large scale streaming motion" and none so far has been able to explain it . . . . The strong implication is that these galaxies in a region hundreds of million of light years across must be pulled by the gravitational forces of some huge, undiscovered mass beyond the range of astronomers' vision . . . . The astronomy of the last few years has brought a surprising realization that the universe is highly organized on a large scale. Galaxies and other masses, instead of being randomly scattered about, seem to fall into clumps and filaments: separated by empty voids, forming frothy structure that is now described as "sponge-like". . . .

The Bentov model was proposed in a descriptive form, as a nonquantitative philosophic overview of cosmology and higher consciousness, and thus reminds one of Emmanuel Kant's anticipation of the modern view of galaxies. Such a qualitative model can play an important role in the advance of cosmology as a source of inspiration and a point of departure.

Consider an analogous situation in recent cosmological thought with the Anthropic Principle. In its strong form, it suggests that life in the universe is impossible, unless the laws of nature are exactly as they have been observed, and the basic physical constants of nature are almost exactly as measured. If things were even slightly different, stars and galaxies would never form, or heavy elements would not exist, or everything would have happened too fast for you and me to exist! Not that these nonstandard universes could not exist, but without intelligent life to observe them, they would be meaningless, almost aborted versions of the real thing.

From such philosophic generalizations, refined in great detail, astrophysicists have been able to deduce certain limits on observable variables, such as ages of stars and galaxies, the strength of gravity, isotropy of matter distribution, and so on.

In an extreme case, the Anthropic Principle leads to the view that an almost unlimited number of universes, adjacent in space and time, could coexist, each with slightly different inhabitants or none at all, and each with slightly different physical laws and conditions. We just happen to exist in one of these universes and are forever prevented from physically communicating with other universes because of space-time factors.

This picture reminds one of the Everett-Wheeler "many worlds" hypothesis, deduced from quantum mechanical considerations, which suggests that our familiar universe is just one of an enormous number of coexisting universes.

It is remarkable that Bentov, in his cosmic visions, formulated a system of multiple coexisting worlds similar to a foam of "bubbles," reflecting different levels of reality, which he equated with levels of consciousness. From smaller cosmoses to ever larger ones, containing the smaller, he finally perceived Manifest Creation, or what he termed "All-there-is," as a holographic pattern of interconnecting information of all levels of creation.

This bubble imagery has found curious expression in a theory formulated in 1986 by a team at the Harvard-Smithsonian Center for Astrophysics. Engaged in a three-dimensional mapping of galactic distribution, they detected a large-scale bubble-like structure: galaxies were found to be located on the surfaces of imaginary spherical shells. The centers of these bubbles were thought to be regions of violent explosions, which flung matter outward in symmetrical spherical waves, seen today as spherical shells of high galactic density, surrounding low matter-density regions.

A more detailed quantitative treatment of Bentov's model is in order, and one of the interesting sources to be explored is the work of Kurt Gödel.

A mathematician and a friend and colleague of Einstein, Gödel developed a unique solution to the equations of the general theory of relativity. His mathematical model contains two features that are of particular relevance to the Bentov model: (1) it describes a rotating universe shaped as a torus or an involuting smoke ring, and (2) in this universe, the world line (space-time trajectory) of a particle or an observer traces a path that closes upon itself in a continuous movement, analogous to the continuous stream of energy-matter from the white hole to the black hole of the Bentov model.

Obviously, many additional data and careful study are necessary to compare Bentov's model with the physical universe. Hopefully, the orbiting space telescope, originally scheduled for August 1986 and now delayed, and other space probes, perhaps unthought of today, will provide the final convincing data.

Edward Apgar received his Ph.D. in physics from Rutgers University. He taught physics at Bennington College and conducted research at the Plasma Physics Laboratory at Princeton University, the National Aeronautics and Space Administration Electronics Research Center, and the National Magnet Laboratory at the Massachusetts Institute of Technology.

About the Author

Itzhak Bentov was born in Czechoslovakia in 1923. During World War II he moved to Israel and in 1954 came to the United States, where he began his career as an inventor and a consultant to industry, eventually specializing in biomedical engineering. He was involved in studying the effects of altered states of consciousness on human physiology, and wrote *Stalking the Wild Pendulum: On the Mechanics of Consciousness*. He died in 1979, leaving the notes for the present book, which his wife, Mirtala, finished.

Sculpture of Ben by Mirtala

Stalking the Wild Pendulum
On the Mechanics of Consciousness
Itzhak Bentov

ISBN 0-89281-202-8 • $12.95 (Can $20.95) pb
208 pages, $5^3/8$ x $8^1/4$

In his exciting and original view of the universe, Itzhak Bentov
has provided a new perspective on human consciousness and its
limitless possibilities. Widely known and loved for his delightful humor and imagination, Bentov explains the familiar world
of phenomena with perceptions that are as lucid as they are thrill-
ing. He gives us a provocative picture of ourselves in an expanded, conscious, holistic universe, showing us that:

- Our bodies mirror the universe, down to the working of
  each cell.

- We are pulsating beings in a vibrating universe, in
  constant motion between the finite and the infinite.

- The universe and all matter is consciousness in the
  process of developing.

- Our brains are thought amplifiers, not thought's source.

- The universe is a hologram. And so is the brain—
  a hologram interpreting a holographic universe.

- We can instantly reclaim any information ever known

"Dazzles the imagination and causes you to rethink everything
you ever thought you knew about the nature of reality."

Jean Houston

This and other Destiny Books/Inner Traditions titles are available
at many fine bookstores, or, to order directly from the publisher,
please send check or money order payable to Inner Traditions for
the total amount, plus $3.50 shipping for the first book and $1.00
for each additional book to:

Inner Traditions, P.O. Box 388, Rochester, VT 05767
Fax (802) 767-3726 • Or call 1-800-246-8648
Visit our Web site: www.InnerTraditions.com

BOOKS OF RELATED INTEREST

Stalking the Wild Pendulum
On the Mechanics of Consciousness
by Itzhak Bentov

The Universe Is a Green Dragon
A Cosmic Creation Story
by Brian Swimme, Ph.D.

Morphic Resonance
The Nature of Formative Causation
by Rupert Sheldrake

Chaos, Creativity, and Cosmic Consciousness
*by Rupert Sheldrake, Terence McKenna,
and Ralph Abraham*

The Presence of the Past
Morphic Resonance and the Habits of Nature
by Rupert Sheldrake

The Secret Teachings of Plants
The Intelligence of the Heart in the
Direct Perception of Nature
by Stephen Harrod Buhner

Science and the Akashic Field
An Integral Theory of Everything
by Ervin Laszlo

The Akashic Experience
Science and the Cosmic Memory Field
by Ervin Laszlo

Inner Traditions • Bear & Company
P.O. Box 388
Rochester, VT 05767
1-800-246-8648
www.InnerTraditions.com

Or contact your local bookseller